Chris Darwin was born in London ▨▨▨▨. After he failed most of his exams at school, his grandmother gave him some advice: 'If you cannot be first, be peculiar'.

Since then he has been a professional rickshaw rider, pizza delivery driver, windsurfing instructor, photographer, labourer, undercover reporter exposing illegal dogfighting for Granada Television, waiter, President of the Aardvark Liberation Front and teaboy in a film company.

He raises money for the National Heart Foundation through the activities of the Social Climbers and lives in Sydney.

John Amy was born in Armidale, New South Wales in 1959. He is a committed non-mountaineer and armchair adventurer. He studied history at the University of New South Wales, worked as a copywriter in advertising and public relations and spent two years mixing business with pleasure as the deputy editor of the *Sydney Morning Herald Good Food Guide*. He is now a freelance writer.

He is moderately well travelled and has spied the Himalayas from a distance but has never set foot above the snowline and has no intention of doing so.

He is a keen golfer and does not own a BMW.

THE
SOCIAL
CLIMBERS

CHRIS DARWIN AND JOHN AMY

SUN
AUSTRALIA

Photographers:
Jonathan Chester (Extreme Images), Chris Darwin, Wolfgang Ebert,
Alison Murphy, Milton Sams, Glen Singleman, Wayne Stead, Trace
Taylor-Young and Neil Watson
Photographic Suppliers:
Custom Darkroom, Peter Dambiec, Duracell, Fuji, Ilford, Photo
Rentals, Richard Wilson Studios and Tecnoprint
Illustrations
Michael Tunica

5% of Chris Darwin's royalties are donated
to the National Heart Foundation of Australia.

First published 1991 by Pan Macmillan Publishers Australia
a division of Pan Macmillan (Australia) Pty Limited
63–71 Balfour Street, Chippendale, Sydney
A.C.N. 001 184 014

National Library of Australia
cataloguing-in-publication data:

Darwin, Chris, 1961–
The social climbers.

ISBN 0 7251 0680 8.

1. Darwin, Chris, 1961–   — Journeys — Andes.
2. Mountaineering — Andes — Humor. 3. Andes –
Description and travel — Humor. I. Amy, John,
1959–   . II. Title.

796.522098

Typeset in 12/14 pt Century Old style by Post Typesetters, Brisbane
Printed in Australia by Australian Print Group

Front cover photographs:
Mt Chopicalqui, 6,345 metres. Photo:CD.
Dinner party on Mt Pisco. Photo: M Sams.

To Ari and Jess, my flatmates,
who helped and encouraged me for three years
but never saw a mountain.

CONTENTS

FOREWORD

It was a sticky summer's day in the central business district of Sydney. I was cursing my choice to work in an office rather than living the carefree life of a mountain vagabond, when through the door walked a very strange man. He wore a bow tie with a rather loud electric blue shirt. For a briefcase he had a white kids' sandwich box with Mickey Mouse stickers on it. My immediate impression was that he was either in advertising or he was just an eccentric. He turned out to be both.

'Hello, I'm Chris Darwin,' he said thrusting his hand out for a firm handshake (something my father always told me was a sign of good character). 'I hear you know something about mountaineering, I must admit it's something I'm not really up on you know, but I would like to organise the world's highest formal dinner party. How would I go about holding one at eight thousand metres?'

I suppose I should not have been surprised by his pommy accent. I had to pinch myself to make sure I wasn't dreaming that I was in some Monty Python sketch. Even if I never met him again he was already leaving an indelible impression on me.

As patiently as I could, I tried to explain to this tall

skinny Englishman that just getting to eight thousand metres is akin to swimming the Channel with one arm or hopping across the Simpson Desert on one leg. Eating is rather difficult too, because being up there makes you feel like you have the worst hangover imaginable.

He listened carefully enough but the seriousness of climbing at high altitude must have eluded him because he continued to pester me for the next few months and before I knew what was happening I was helping him arrange what would surely be the most unusual suicide case in history.

He and his friends were actually going ahead with their plan and I was only successful in curbing their mad caper by bringing the altitude down to a still dangerous six or seven thousand metres. No climbing up the pavements for this lot, they were going to do the real thing and make it even harder by taking chairs and tables up there too.

The very worst thing though, was that they wanted me along with them. To get out of this very difficult position, I hatched a brilliant plan. I went to live on the other side of Australia and began organising another expedition to Everest — nothing but the highest mountain was going to be a good enough excuse. By the skin of my teeth I avoided going. As it turned out it was just as well: the wine froze, the food was tinned and I understand they had to stack their own plates (just quietly we don't stack on Everest).

To be serious, the Social Climbers as they called themselves, showed us that no matter how silly an idea, if the people are sillier, it will be accomplished. This is an earnestly silly book about a gravely batty idea which turned very serious.

Tim Macartney-Snape
October 1990.
(Still safely in Meekatharra, far Western Australia, in order to avoid a possible sequel.)

INTRODUCTION AND ACKNOWLEDGEMENTS

This is a non-mountaineer's mountaineering book. I have written about events as I saw them and I hope the expedition members can forgive the directness of my account.

There are no angels or devils in this book, just normal people under considerable mental and physical stress, behaving very differently from how they would normally act. I decided, rather than conveniently sweeping the arguments, selfishness and jealousy under the carpet, I would record them beside the humour, camaraderie and enjoyment.

The intention is to narrate the story in a light-hearted but raw form. The book is like the control panel in a plane, presenting all the data. It is up to the reader to interpret the information and fly the book.

Most readers probably imagine they are incapable of climbing a mountain. By the end of the book I hope to have convinced you that, with the right training and motivation, you could have reached the summit of ours.

The Social Climbers, guides, porters and documentary crew put a staggering amount of work into the project and I apologise if any of them feel this account does not reflect their level of commitment. To give a balanced view of events I have been very fortunate to have been able to use the expedition members' diaries, tapes and documentary material. Many of the quotes are very personal and I hope the contributors feel I have not betrayed their confidence in me.

I wish to express my sincere thanks to *Ansett Airlines*, who saved the expedition, and all the other sponsors and individuals listed in the back of the book who helped turn a ridiculous idea into a ludicrous reality.

I would like to thank everyone who helped with the book including the book committee (also listed in the back), the staff at Pan Macmillan, and John Amy and Jessica Block, who tamed my ravings into a publishable form.

Chris Darwin
November 1990.
(Sydney)

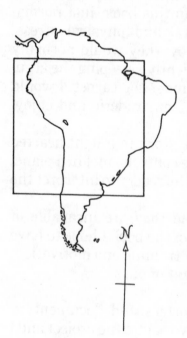

The Social Climbers
SOUTH AMERICA

ENGLAND

1
ORIGIN OF THE
SOCIAL CLIMBERS

If you cannot be first, be peculiar.

Grandmother's advice to author aged thirteen

Nervously I glanced down into the crevasse.

It looked as beautiful as I knew it was dangerous. A carved blue-white vertical wall of ice, adorned with massive icicles, plunging into the depths. It was so deep I could not see the bottom. I knew a fall into it without a safety rope would mean certain death.

I had already abseiled down a thirty metre ice wall. There was only one route over the crevasse, across a narrow ramp of snow and ice called a snow bridge.

Milton Sams, our head guide, watched me from the far side of the snow bridge. His green duvet jacket hood partly shrouded his unshaven face but I could see he looked concerned. He had already saved my life once on the expedition.

Behind him, there was an unbroken panorama of snow-capped Andean peaks stretching sixty kilometres. We were at 5500 metres on Mt Pisco in Peru. The Social Climbers were evacuating the mountain after a successful dress rehearsal for the world's highest dinner party.

We were all exhausted, none of us had washed for two weeks, we smelt disgusting and were almost out of food. I hated crevasses.

3

The snow bridge was only half a metre wide. On each side, it fell away vertically into the depths of the crevasse. I relaxed momentarily and made the mistake of peering over the edge.

'Steady, Chris, don't look down,' warned Milton.

A more experienced mountaineer would have paused to regain his balance. But I was inexperienced and in a hurry to reach safety. Like most accidents, everything seemed to happen in slow motion. I stepped on the snow bridge and my left foot sank into the snow deeper than I expected. The weight of my pack pulled me sideways. For a second I was frozen, teetering on my left leg. Then, ever so gently, I started to topple into the crevasse.

Seven years before I had also fallen off a bridge. Not a snow bridge but Chiswick Bridge over the Thames in London.

Chiswick Bridge lies just beyond the finishing line of the historic Oxford and Cambridge Boat Race. Every year for the last 160 years, thousands of screaming supporters have lined the banks cheering on their respective eights. It is an exhausting race to row but generally uneventful to watch. One crew usually wins easily so the media are always on the lookout for interesting angles.

In 1982 they got one. A struggling band called the Turkeys of Sloane decided to stage a publicity stunt to promote their first and only single, 'OK Ya'. This biting parody of Sloane Rangers had crawled its way up to 140 in the charts. The band knew that as the two crews crossed the finishing line, every television and press camera would home in on Chiswick Bridge.

At that moment lead singer 'Turkey' Somerset would leap off the bridge, roped-up and dressed as a turkey, with 'OK Ya' emblazoned across his fowl breast. The resulting publicity would surely create a hit record.

On the day, things did not go according to plan. Fully costumed, roped-up and ready to go, with the competing

4

crews only minutes away, Turkey chickened out.

'I can't do it,' he whispered in terror. 'I can't stand heights.'

The opportunity would soon be lost. A replacement turkey had to be found. Turkey desperately looked at his two-man support crew standing on the crowded bridge. Neither were willing or suitable. Hugo Spowers, from the Dangerous Sports Club, had recently been arrested for bungy jumping. The courts would not take kindly to a second offence. Alex was an illegal immigrant from Spain who had fled to avoid National Service. If caught by the police, he faced deportation and a stint in the army.

I had been hired as the photographer for the stunt. Shouting above the roar of the crowd, Turkey asked me if I would take his place. I felt a bit sorry for him. It was obvious he had been carried away in a wave of bravado when planning it and had simply ignored his fear of heights. Caught up in the excitement of the moment, I stupidly agreed.

Hurriedly, I climbed into the turkey outfit, attached the ropes and leapt into the unknown. On the way down I prayed they had got the length of the rope right. I plunged ten metres before the elastic rope pulled me up with a jolt a few metres above the Thames. I flapped madly on cue.

I wasn't the only one in a flap. Just then a BBC commentator looked at his monitor. He thought I was hanging myself and announced with horror that someone appeared to be committing suicide. The police did not know what I was doing but agreed I was committing something, most likely a crime.

The two exhausted crews drifted past me, too dazed to acknowledge a madman in a turkey suit. I started to climb back up the rope but was stopped short by the voice of authority, amplified through a loud hailer.

'Please come down, sir,' boomed a police officer, in a long-suffering but polite tone.

Squinting through my turkey mask I saw, to my horror, a small police boat below me.

'I'm all right thanks officer, it's easier to go up,' I shouted down cheerfully, to disguise my attempted escape.

Turkey leaned over the edge of the bridge above and warned me against trying to make my getaway.

'Give up, Chris. The policeman here is going to cut the rope unless you go down.'

The boos and hisses from the crowd made it clear whose side they were on and did not improve the disposition of the bobbies. But cutting the rope was not a sensible option because I would very likely crash through the bottom of the police boat waiting below. I wondered what the penalty was for sinking a police vessel? The officer clearly did not relish the prospect of being sunk in midwinter by a falling turkey. He demanded I give up.

'Sir,' he shouted, losing his patience, 'if you don't come down in thirty seconds I will also charge you with attempting to evade arrest.'

I was stunned. I had done many stupid things in my life but had never actually been arrested. One year I caused a minor stampede of shoppers when I plastered fifty-per-cent sale signs over the windows of Harrods department store. However I always hoped people would accept these pranks in the way they were intended: not malicious, just harmless fun.

Sadly the policeman in the boat below did not see it that way. I climbed down, was arrested and taken away.

Next day I appeared in court charged with breach of the peace. The court case was pure farce.

'Mr Darwin,' the police officer told the magistrate, 'was in breach of the peace because he was flapping and making squawking noises.'

My defence was also wafer thin. I tried to convince the magistrate that by squawking and flapping I was only behaving the way a real turkey would, if hung from a bridge, an argument in which I had no confidence. So I tried another tack. Surely the boat race was hardly a peaceful event anyway?

Amazingly the magistrate accepted this reasoning. She said, with a smile, that there were more pressing cases to hear and asked me to refrain from jumping off bridges dressed as any kind of animal in future. I could not believe my luck.

The record didn't fare as well. Despite national TV coverage and several newspaper articles it fell, like a turkey with clipped wings, right out of the charts.

Photography at that time was not my only career. I also moonlighted in my own business, London Rickshaw Tours. For six pounds fifty, I bicycled tourists around Trafalgar Square, Buckingham Palace and Westminster.

Unfortunately the combined weights of well-fed American tourists and their expensive camera equipment proved too much for my Achilles tendon. I was put into plaster for two months and the rickshaw service folded.

During my convalescence, Turkey often visited to relieve my boredom. We discovered we had something in common. Celibacy.

Neither of us could afford to take girls out to expensive restaurants, so we decided to hold a picnic at night. As we discussed it, the concept developed. What started off as a picnic became an elaborate formal dinner held outdoors, complete with borrowed dining room table and chairs. The Dining Out Club was born.

The Dining Out Club's first dinner was one of the best. The location was modest. A small wooded park beside the Thames. I had told Henrietta, a girl I was fond of, that we were going to a restaurant.

Since it was a mild summer evening, I suggested we take a short cut through the park to the fictitious restaurant. She immediately spotted the beautifully laid-out dining table in a small glade overlooking the river. When she went to investigate she was ambushed by a butler offering champagne, who turned out to be a close friend. Henrietta burst out laughing, delighted by the joke.

It was an exceptional evening. Dinner for six by the Thames. The surprise created a romantic mood but the evening was not without a twist. After dinner, the women insisted we go for a walk while they stayed at the table. After our return, we continued chatting as before.

Suddenly Turkey exclaimed, 'They're stark naked.'

In our absence they had stripped. Due to the dim candlelight and the fact that the girls had been wearing low-cut dresses, none of us had even noticed.

Dining Out Club dinners were always a total surprise to the women we asked. They were lured to the location under false pretences. Dress was always black tie, purely to enhance the visual effect of a formal dinner party in an incongruous setting. Where necessary, evening gowns and dinner suits were hung on a clothes rail beside the table for us to change into when we arrived.

The locations became increasingly bizarre in our attempts to outdo each previous dinner. Venues included a secluded island in the middle of a river in Wales, the international departure lounge of London Airport, a ski slope in France, and a diving platform in the North Sea. Ironically, they cost far more in the end than a night at an expensive restaurant.

I never found earning a living as a photographer easy. To pay the bills I took on any photographic assignment: weddings, parties, even portraits of dogs.

My first big break came with an expedition. I was invited to be the official photographer for the first solo attempt to windsurf around Britain.

The starting line for the Round Britain Windsurf was at Tower Bridge in London. Hundreds of well-wishers, sponsors, media hacks and dignitaries assembled to cheer Tim Batstone on the first leg of his 3000 kilometre voyage. Unfortunately, someone had miscalculated the tides in the Thames. In the flukey wind, Tim fell off his board and was swept upstream by the strong currents.

The press had a field day. After all if he could not even cross the starting line what chance would he have in the open ocean?

He did make it, raised forty thousand pounds for the Royal National Lifeboats Institution and earned a place in *The Guinness Book of Records*. I spent ten weeks bouncing along in a five metre rubber duck chasing him through some of the world's most treacherous waters and the second largest whirlpool in the world — the Gulf of Corrievrechan off Scotland.

Monstrous seas made good press copy but in fact we spent more time becalmed. We would sit for hours waiting for the wind in the middle of a glassy ocean, drinking coffee and enjoying being far away from civilisation.

It gave me a taste of what expeditions are like: long periods of discomfort and boredom offset by moments of excitement, the solitude and the enormous sense of achievement.

After the expedition I decided to get in on the ground floor of the film industry. I took a job as a tea boy with a film company. I was serving a boardroom lunch when the managing director mentioned to a journalist from the advertising magazine *Campaign* that I was Charles Darwin's great-great-grandson. The journalist found it very amusing that a direct descendant of one of the seminal thinkers of the nineteenth century had managed to fail his biology exam at school and was now employed as a tea boy. He wrote an article about me.

Unfortunately that was the high point of my career in the British film industry. My prospects for promotion were hampered by a couple of glaring errors. I reversed a film truck over the bonnet of my producer's car while she was in it. Shortly afterwards, during a Heinz Beans commercial spoofing *Beau Geste* and the French Foreign Legion, I failed to notice the camels eating the director's afternoon-tea cream cakes.

After a year and a half with the same company I was going nowhere fast. I was in a rut and needed to make a radical move. Australia, I had heard, had a wonderful outdoor lifestyle and a booming film industry.

My contact at *Campaign* proved useful. I asked him if they would be interested in a feature article on Australian advertising. They agreed, I wrote the article and Australia became my home.

AUSTRALIA

2
LEARNING TO
PRONOUNCE
MT HUASCARAN

I do wish all the thermally-clad munchers every success and good fortune.

HRH Prince Charles

T he range of possibilities of doing something exceptional in life are enormous: politics, business, sport, science, entertainment or religion. There was nothing exceptional about my year in Australian advertising. Work was regular but again I felt dissatisfied.

I wanted to do something different. A single achievement which stood by itself and was amusing, worthwhile and impressive. The idea of an expedition excited me. I had learned from the Round Britain Windsurf that they can be self-contained, self-financing and enormously satisfying.

Over a period of months I had a number of ideas. All of them were impractical, but three appealed to me.

The first idea was to hang-glide across Australia being towed by my mini moke. The second was to sell advertising space for charity on an old tin bath and then put it into orbit around the earth. The third was to stage a dinner party on the summit of one of the highest mountains in the world.

All these concepts had major problems. However, I had experience of holding dinners in remote locations for the Dining Out Club. The world's highest formal dinner fitted my criteria for an expedition: amusing, worthwhile and impressive.

The concept was like a collision between Monty Python and Scott of the Antarctic. I envisaged a group of people wearing black tie or ball dresses sitting at a dinner table and being served by a butler, while surrounded by snow-capped peaks. A surreal image.

The expedition could be made worthwhile if we raised money for charity in the process and climbing a high mountain would be an impressive achievement in itself.

In my more naive moments I believed that it would be easy to organise. We would simply go to Nepal, hire a couple of guides, climb a mountain, have the dinner and go home. My laughable enthusiasm rubbed off on a friend, Al Darling, who agreed to help with the organisation. We christened ourselves the Social Climbers and set to work.

We decided to test the water by sending a letter to *The Guinness Book of Records*. Would they recognise this as a legitimate world record? The answer was yes.

A second letter was sent to Prince Charles, asking for his official support. Again we received a positive response:

> Dear Mr Darwin,
> Your wonderfully eccentric expedition is full of potential — both humorous and financial — and I do wish all the thermally-clad munchers every success and good fortune. Please send me a photograph of the achievement.
> Charles

So we had a potential world record and support from the future King of Britain. All we needed now was a high mountain. We pored over my school atlas and were encouraged. All the mountains appeared very attainable. The selection process was not so simple. For our world record to stand for any length of time, the mountain must be closer in height to Mt Everest (8848 metres), than Mt Kosciusko (2173 metres). The fact that neither of us had ever mountaineered or been above 2500 metres — and that was by cable car on a skiing holiday — did not worry us.

New Zealand's Mt Cook (3765 metres), was too small. Mont Blanc, Europe's highest peak at 4886 metres, was too low again. Mt Kilimanjaro (5896 metres), and Mt McKinley (6195 metres), the highest summits in Africa and North America, still seemed undersized. Only a Himalayan or Andean peak would do.

We decided that 8000 metres, a nice round number, was the magic figure. Anything above that height sounded truly impressive. We checked and found there were fourteen mountains in the world above that altitude — surely one of them must be climbable by a totally inexperienced team of inspired amateurs?

Sydney's mountaineering fraternity did not share our optimism. Every mountaineer politely told us we were a disaster waiting to happen. Then we met Tim Macartney-Snape.

Tim holds four Everest records. He is the first Australian to climb Everest, the first person to walk from sea level to the top of Everest, the first man with a double-barrelled surname to climb Everest and the first person to hold three Everest records.

Tim was also the first mountaineer to take us seriously. Most people think of mountaineers as bearded monsters. Rough, gruff types. Tim is exactly the opposite. Tall, wiry, thin-faced, even a little ill-looking, he is also calm and reserved with an understated wit.

It was Tim who convinced us to lower our sights to the 6800 metre mark. There were seventy-six peaks in the world above that height, surely now we were spoilt for choice. Also, he introduced us to Milton Sams. A builder by trade, Milton is the most experienced South American mountaineering guide in Australia.

I arranged to meet him in Tim's office. He could not have looked more out of place surrounded by fax machines, photocopiers and padded swivel chairs.

Milton resembles everybody's idea of a mountaineer.

15

The size of a small delivery van, he has huge shoulders, a big, rounded red nose and a curly mop of brown hair: definitely someone to have on your side in a barroom brawl. We sat on the grass opposite Tim's office, eating a couple of ham sandwiches and discussing mountaineering. He explained that the biggest problem facing commercial mountaineering is the public's perception that the sport is only accessible to bearded supermen. He obviously considered that if he could coax, push and cajole a group of total novices up a high mountain for a dinner, the resulting publicity would help undermine the myth and boost his business.

'So, er, why do you want to climb a 6800 metre mountain?' he asked prising a piece of ham fat from between his teeth with his little finger. 'There is no record for the highest dinner party so why not choose something a little smaller, a bit easier, say around the 6000 metre mark.'

I explained that the Mera peak (6400 metres) in Nepal had been suggested and I did not want to go any lower. The very mention of Nepal made his eyes narrow. Nepal was in direct competition with the Andes and attracted most of the mountaineers and trekkers.

'I suppose you could try Huascaran,' he said doubtfully, almost thinking out loud. 'Just below 6800 metres.' He was obviously concerned about the whole plan and we agreed he should think it over.

I immediately liked him, he was so different from all the other neat, precise often condescending mountaineers. For starters, his clothing looked like it had just been savaged by a pack of wolves. Although he realised I knew nothing about mountaineering, he listened patiently to my ideas. I felt we would work well together.

He had a slightly embarrassed and clumsy way of talking. He often sounded like he was expressing several ideas simultaneously, but that did not worry me as I could see the underlying logic was always sound.

16

When I next spoke to him on the phone he had obviously resolved all his concerns.

'Mount Huascaran is our mountain, no worries,' he promised enthusiastically. 'It is the seventh highest mountain in the world outside the Himalayas and the highest mountain in Peru. Anyone would be pushing shit uphill to have a dinner party any higher. There's no technical mountaineering required. It's a straight bloody walk to the top.'

Listening to Milton made it seem as if all the other experts had been unnecessarily pessimistic about our chances. His patience and willingness to spend hours advising me on the expedition immediately made him a vital asset. In any event, he was virtually the only mountaineer who would give us the time of day. I was prepared to believe anyone who said the project was possible. Anyone who was negative, I simply ignored. We made a booking for nine people for Peru in May 1988. From what Milton said, the hardest part of climbing Huascaran was pronouncing its name correctly (Whoosschaaran).

I have no doubt that if someone could have predicted the hardships we would encounter and the injuries we would sustain: two cases of hypothermia, one of malaria, eight cases of a stomach infection called giardia, two cracked ribs, a ripped shoulder, bronchitis, an ulcer, five cases of piles, one pregnancy and a frozen bottle of Hardy's red wine, I would have cancelled the project.

Did they fib to Hillary as well?

We had our mountain, but we still had no one to climb it. None of Sydney's mountaineers were even remotely interested in coming. They found our lighthearted approach to their sport irreverent, and were totally underwhelmed by our startling lack of experience.

'A dinner party at that altitude is impossible,' said one mountaineer. 'It is like climbing Everest in thongs.' We got knock back after knock back.

We lowered our sights and decided to accept anyone who showed the slightest interest in the project. Lots of non-mountaineers thought the concept of climbing an enormous peak in a remote country for the sole purpose of holding a dinner party, sounded like fun. The expedition slowly grew from two to seven members, then quickly dropped back to two. People either lost interest in the project when I tried to stop them just dining out on the idea and get them to do some work as well, or they proved totally unfit. I knew I was in trouble when my founding co-member, Al, also dropped out, after we had a blazing row.

It now looked as if the expedition was going to be dinner for one, with Milton as my witness. Either that or cancel the expedition. I cancelled and the Social Climbers sank without trace. Virtually no one noticed.

There was, however, one person who kept the concept alive. Neil Watson was both a good friend and a great supporter of the project. He had no intention of going himself and explained his reasons.

> *I remember finishing* Everest The Hard Way *by Chris Bonington and I thought, 'That is amazing, that is incredible, I never, ever want to do anything like that in my life. Why on earth would you want to put yourself through that kind of torture?'*

An English lawyer in his mid twenties, Neil is a fitness fanatic and triathlete. He has a whippet-like frame, neatly-cut brown hair, round John Lennon glasses and claims he looks like Tom Cruise although the resemblance is lost on me. At the time he seemed a classic yuppie: a Cambridge University post-graduate, with a well-heeled job in corporate finance and a Saab Turbo.

He had a talent that I knew was my weakness. He was a great motivator. His motor-mouth wit, self-confidence and enthusiasm made people follow him. Eventually he talked me into continuing with the expedition and I talked him into joining it.

18

He later claimed he wanted to come because he liked the idea of being in *The Guinness Book of Records*. Since his only talent was eating, the world's highest dinner was his best chance. But the truth was very different.

He was bored with his job. The idea of the dinner party appealed to his sense of the absurd and mountaineering offered a new, radically different challenge. Apparently unconcerned about his complete lack of mountaineering experience, he assured me, as the world's greatest arm-chair mountaineer, that the expedition could not do without him. He was right — I would need his support to rebuild it.

Most expedition books give the impression that a group of people wake up one morning, decide to climb Everest or walk to the Pole, ring up a couple of potential sponsors, bank a few fat cheques and set off bound for glory. We soon discovered nothing could be further from the truth.

Organising an expedition is an unmitigated nightmare. Expeditions are one-per-cent thrashing around on the mountain and ninety-nine-per-cent sitting at a word processor or on the telephone, being told 'no'. It took just under two years to prepare for a dinner which only lasted twenty minutes. It was far harder to organise to climb the mountain than it was to climb the bloody thing.

Why? Because economic reality dictated that we had to organise everything for free or at least at an enormous discount. If we had paid commercial rates for all of our eighty-six sponsored products and services — Aerolineas Argentinas air fares and freight, accommodation, ultra-light dining furniture and accessories, mountaineering equipment, formal wear, and the rest — as well as employed the sixty-one part-time helpers, the total bill would have exceeded half a million dollars. Fine if the National Geographic Society was picking up the tab but otherwise impractical. One glance at the list of sponsors in the appendix will explain why expeditions are an endangered species unless heavily subsidised.

We had created a monster. I was forced to give up my job to work on the project full-time, earning a wage only as a waiter or delivering pizzas at night. But still there was too much work. We needed more help.

Neil convinced Eddie Moore, a twenty-four-year-old accountant at the Sheraton Wentworth Hotel, to join me. Eddie tossed in his job and began to work full-time on the project, too.

Eddie was also a fitness fanatic and triathlete. He looked more like a surfer than a potential mountaineer. Blond haired, blue eyed and handsome, Eddie had a naturally laid-back personality. Wherever the fun was, Eddie was.

His many achievements included setting a new record on the Channel 10 dating programme, 'Perfect Match'. He went on television to try and find suitable women partners for the expedition. He and his date were sent away to Ayers Rock and during that weekend Eddie exerted his considerable charms over both his perfect match and the glamorous chaperone. But charm alone could not convince either of them to come on the expedition.

We did have more luck in other areas. An adventure film company, Orana Films, agreed to make a documentary on the expedition. The National Heart Foundation was delighted to accept our offer to raise funds on their behalf.

In our efforts to find a butler for the dinner I wrote to every distinguished-looking actor over fifty in Sydney. Eddie Ash was the only one who responded but he was perfect for the part. Small, slightly built with grey hair, Eddie was a sixty-two-year-old grandfather who passionately wanted to climb a mountain.

He looked much younger than his age, was extraordinarily fit and had the energy of an eight-year-old. Always positive, always smiling, he never had a bad word to say about anyone.

He started his working life doing headstands on the

flying trapeze in the circus and was now an actor. His reason for coming on the expedition was simple. At his age he felt this would be his last opportunity to climb a high mountain, an ambition he had harboured for decades. We renamed him Ballantyne after a chocolate sponsor, Ballantyne's Entertainmints. He vowed to give up alcohol until he had climbed Huascaran and threw himself into the expedition organisation, especially the Heart Foundation fundraising, with an energy and determination that I have rarely witnessed.

There were two main obstacles to the expedition. Finding the right women was proving to be a mini-Everest in itself. Furthermore we still did not have a major sponsor. The companies we approached were more inclined to question the authenticity of Prince Charles's letter than to actually put up any money. No one believed the expedition would happen.

Clearly we had to do something dramatic to launch the Social Climbers, to publicise our search for women and attract a major sponsor. We knew that to attract the media we either had to publicly humiliate ourselves or risk life and limb. We decided to do both.

The plan was to lower a dining-room table off the aptly named Fear Overhang, at Sydney's North Head. Neil, Eddie, Tim Macartney-Snape and I would abseil down and be served a necessarily light lunch at our suspended table by Ballantyne.

3
A FLAWLESS
FLOOR–LESS LUNCH

Easy. The trick is making it
one-hundred-per-cent safe
but looking lethal.

Tadd Pride

It is easy to say you are going to hang a table off an eighty metre cliff, have four people in black tie abseil down to be served lunch, with wine, by a sixty-two-year-old butler while being filmed from helicopters hovering no more than twenty metres away. The hard part is not killing yourself.

We persuaded Sydney's best rigging/stunt/explosive/ 'we will do anything you can think of' company — Pride Effects — to help. Tadd Pride looks like an American version of Billy Connolly, only scruffier. Nothing fazes him.

'Easy', he said when I showed him the cliff. He calmly puffed on his twentieth non-filtered cigarette of the day. 'The trick is making it one-hundred-per-cent safe but looking lethal.'

North Head is Sydney's most spectacular cliff at the entrance to Sydney Harbour. To the right there are superb views up the harbour to the Sydney skyline.

Crashing waves eighty metres below the overhanging cliff, create a startling impression. The rock you are standing on appears to be floating in thin air high above the sea. Many tortured souls choose to commit suicide there.

On the morning of 17 March 1989 I arrived at the Fear Overhang at five. It was still dark. I sat on a rock near the

22

cliff watching the orange glow over the sea strengthen as the day dawned. I felt like a groom on his wedding day: doubts were creeping in.

This was make-or-break day for the Social Climbers. If anything went wrong someone could easily be killed, the press would be there in force and would crucify me. It would all be over before it had even started.

The rig was very simple. A few pieces of scaffolding extending out from the cliff were held in place by half a kilometre of rope in a spaghetti-like configuration, anchoring the rig to an enormous rock.

We had taken every possible precaution. A security guard had been posted overnight to guard the rig. I wandered over to check with him that no one had tampered with it. He was sound asleep.

Tadd had been very successful in making the rig look lethal. But I had no idea whether the second requirement had been fulfilled. Was it one-hundred-per-cent safe? It was too late now to inspect every centimetre of rope for signs of vandalism. The show had to go on regardless.

Television crews, newspaper reporters, radio journalists and well-wishers arrived at ten that morning. Neil had written me a suitably inspiring speech.

'Most of you have been lured here by the prospect of witnessing the world's first free-falling formal luncheon,' I recited clumsily. 'All I can say is I hope you will be disappointed.

'Climbing a 6768 metre mountain with all the equipment necessary for a formal luncheon is the equivalent of walking up a 250 metre tower twenty-seven times with only one lung, carrying the average Great Dane. Yes, it sounds like a nightmare. Why do we do it?'

I told the media about the Heart Foundation and explained why hosting the world's highest formal meal without women would be like drinking champagne without bubbles. And I announced that within the last twenty-four hours we had obtained a major sponsor, Cointreau. I would live to regret that premature sponsorship announcement.

We prepared to descend while four TV helicopters jostled for filming positions like something out of *Apocalypse Now*. Photographers and TV crews also lined the cliff to get the best angles. Disconcertingly, some of the cameramen practised tilting their cameras down to the rocks below, in readiness for a fall.

We were all terrified. Even the most hardened adrenalin addict would have been frightened. Neil and Eddie had learned to abseil only a few weeks before and that was over a nine metre cliff. No wonder they were scared. Just to get to the abseiling position required a tightrope walk, wearing slippery black shoes, along a piece of scaffolding protruding over the cliff edge.

Neil was the guinea pig to test the rig. He painstakingly edged his way along the scaffolding. Despite obvious nerves, he tipped his top hat for the cameras and somehow managed a toothy smile before disappearing over the edge. Later he recorded his fear.

> *My main concern was executing this stunt without executing myself. I was trying to give an aura of total confidence but inside my heart was pounding at two hundred per minute. I looked down to the rocks below and wondered if I would ever see my family again.*

Eddie was the next in line. Unlike Neil he made no effort to disguise his fear. His whole body was taut as he gripped onto the scaffolding with unnecessary force. His wide-eyed expression showed his extreme nervousness. He was aware of nothing around him except the rig, the rope and the rocks below. He hesitated at the far end of the scaffolding, glanced around at me, realised he had no choice and lowered himself over the edge.

Tim Macartney-Snape seemed very composed. He strode along the scaffolding and confidently abseiled out of sight.

24

It was now my turn. I peered over the edge of the cliff. I had that sickening feeling so many people get with heights: an urge to jump. I started shuffling along the scaffolding. Three very worried faces looked up at me from the table fourteen metres below. I took a deep breath, let go of the rig and abseiled down to the table. The Fear Overhang was living up to its name.

The atmosphere at the table was understandably tense. As helicopters flew past and camera motor-drives whirred, Tim tried to calm us with genial chitchat, with talk of frostbite and horrific mountaineering conditions on Everest. He failed miserably to calm our frayed nerves.

'High altitude mountaineering is like running a marathon with the worst hangover imaginable,' he said.

'If it is so terrible, why do it?' we asked.

He was not given a chance to answer. One of our documentary cameramen was lowered down with a hastily written script.

'Gentlemen, I give you the Social Climbers expedition to Peru,' I recited. 'We hope to raise dining etiquette to new peaks and, as my ancestor might have said, "survival of the fattest".'

It took me ten takes to get that short speech right as the cameraman swung precariously beside the table. Everybody started to question my acting ability. I started to have serious doubts about the script.

Momentarily we were left in peace and we began to relax a little. After all, the only difference between this event and a normal black-tie lunch was the absence of a floor. Or so we tried to convince ourselves.

Feeling more confident, we began to look down and around. We watched, fascinated, as the sewage slick from the North Head Sewage Plant moved inexorably towards Australia's most famous beach, Bondi. It looked like a huge brown tongue in the cool blue water.

The media loves accidents and I knew it was vital to give

them one. Ballantyne, our butler, was winched down resplendent in his Grace Bros butler's uniform, carrying a tray of food for lunch. Halfway down he appeared to be struck by a fit of terror and 'accidentally' upset his tray. Our trout narrowly missed us at the table and fell towards the rocks below.

Now it was time for the interviews. A glamorous television presenter was lowered down to the table, shouting at us not to look up her dress. She scooped everyone with an exclusive tableside interview.

Her less brave male colleagues insisted we come to them. ABC TV asked for me to be winched up, a process which took several minutes. They then realised that Tim Macartney-Snape was part of the team and requested an interview. In one fluid movement, born of years of training, Tim appeared to defy gravity as he ascended the rope. I watched in amazement and frustration as he overtook me. By the time I scrambled over the top of the cliff, Tim's interview was over and the best lines were gone.

Slowly the media dispersed and Eddie and Neil climbed back up. We were sunburnt and starving. So over-zealous had Ballantyne been with his fish-dropping antics that no food got near our plates.

By the evening we all felt exhausted from the stress of the day. Thank God it was over.

The North Head launch was a staggering media success, broadcast on every national television network that night and picked up in many newspapers the next day. Overall we featured in twelve television spots, including American TV, thirty-one newspaper and magazine articles and a dozen radio interviews. The coverage extended as far afield as Germany, England, Italy, America, Singapore and China.

All the media reports gently ripped us apart. We were dubbed 'Climbing Cads', 'Wacky Diners' and 'Sydney Toffs'. Other articles were headed 'Mission Ridiculous',

'Lifestyles of the rich and fatuous' and 'Climb every mountain, burp!'

The best piece was undoubtedly in London's *Club International* men's magazine, opposite 'Busty Polly', who claimed to 'put bloody great stonkers on most of the nation's male population'. I don't know what a stonker is but *Club* made some bloody great errors.

'Nutter's Corner' was the title. The picture caption stated:

'These chinless pinbrains are dangling 250 feet above the water at a place called Fear Overhang in northern New Zealand... The four wags were served by their faithful butler Hovis who had to shin up and down with champagne and salmon. Hovis is 68. We just wonder why he didn't cut them loose.'

At least they got the bit about chinless pinbrains right.

4
MOUNTAINS OF WORK

If it was easy, everyone would do it.

Ballantyne

Next day the phone rang hot with women wanting to come on the expedition. No one could hope to get a guernsey without a minimum donation of twenty dollars to the Heart Foundation. We openly admitted that anyone donating one hundred dollars would automatically get an interview.

I knew from reading mountaineering books that expeditions are always stressful and dangerous. People are forced to live in cramped conditions, frequently hungry, thirsty and cold, and pushing themselves beyond their normal limits. All of these factors combined will eat away at morale, causing splinter groups and in-fighting.

We needed four women, all fit, with guts, preferably team players, and, most important, with a sense of humour. Judging by the resumés we received we were spoilt for choice. We quickly realised there were many women far better qualified to climb mountains than we were, a fact repeatedly proved during the expedition.

Of the fifty applicants I gave twenty-odd an interview and basic fitness test. Then I handed them over to Murf, universally known as the 'torturous bastard', to put them under stress and see how they coped.

Derek Murphy, 'Murf', had been recruited as the final male Social Climber and our mountaineering trainer. He was a senior instructor at the Australian School of Mountaineering and had climbed mountains all over the world. He openly admitted that he had climbed so many peaks he was getting bored with bagging summits. But the idea of training a group of no-hopers (his description), to climb a 6800 metre mountain for a dinner party appealed to his sense of humour, especially since he claimed the only time he had ever worn a black tie was at his wedding.

A carpenter by trade, he spent seven years as a sergeant in the commandos and it showed. He was all bark and no bite. He enjoyed pretending he had an abusive, parade-ground mentality but underneath he was a softie. The most important things in his life were his wife and baby boy, closely followed by his bushy moustache and rounded belly.

He was short, squat and powerfully built. Whereas Milton was a genuine rough diamond, Murf was a caricature of the beer-swilling ocker. He genuinely loved teaching, which was fortunate because we had a lot to learn. He was a breath of fresh air after all the other long-faced mountaineers.

'Heaven,' he claimed, 'is somewhere youse can get drunk every night and wake up without a hangover.'

During weekends in the Blue Mountains, west of Sydney, Murf revelled in setting horrific trials for each group of unsuspecting females. These torture tests involved abseiling over waterfalls, strenuous bushwalks in the rain carrying packs laden with rocks and telephone directories, and climbing vertical cliffs. Throughout the trials Murf maintained a constant stream of abuse to undermine each individual's confidence and self-esteem.

Avril Wynne stood out in the initial group of four women Murf tested. The first things I noticed about Avril were her forearms. Women do not put on muscle bulk as easily as men, so you can judge a woman's strength by muscle tone.

29

Avril was obviously strong. We watched, impressed, as she abseiled through a fifteen metre waterfall without a moment's hesitation. 'Either she's got a lot of courage or she's totally stupid,' Neil whispered to me.

It was the last time we saw her that day. While Neil and I struggled through waterfalls at the rear of the group, Avril was far ahead, challenging Murf for the lead. By the end of the day she was the clear favourite.

Apart from her fitness we liked her personality. She never complained and spent the whole time laughing. But it was the name of her dog that finally convinced us she was right for the expedition. Anyone who would call a pet Fart obviously had a perverse sense of humour and belonged at a dinner party at 6800 metres.

Avril was an attractive twenty-eight-year-old, slim, with short dark hair cut in a tomboy style, and a ready smile. When she was not freelancing as a stuntwoman on such films as *Mad Max II* and *The Man From Snowy River II*, she moonlighted as an artificial inseminator on a poultry farm. It was a profession which often proved more dangerous than the stunt work — she carried a length of pipe in her gumboot to hold angry cockerels at bay.

Raised on a property in central New South Wales, she exhibited a kind of bush resilience. She looked on the expedition as a bit of a laugh, as well as an opportunity to see how far her mind could push her body. She was one of the most relaxed people I've ever met, so relaxed I sometimes wondered how she ever got anything done. But she did. It was immediately obvious Avril was not a leader, which was fortunate because we already had far too many chiefs.

Back at base camp in Sydney, two of the chiefs were not working well together. Eddie Moore and I had a fundamentally different approach to every aspect of the expedition organisation. I felt he was a little relaxed about detail and suspected he was not totally committed. He made it very clear what he thought about me.

Darwin is pedantic to the extreme. He is over the top with his planning. He is a crackpot, eccentric weirdo.

As the workload built up so did the tension, the working relationship deteriorated and communication virtually ceased.

The situation was saved by a petite skinny Englishwoman by the name of Tracey Taylor-Young. She appeared on my doorstep wearing Ken Done bike shorts and dripping with sweat. At twenty-nine she still had the enthusiasm and figure of a teenage girl. She had fiery brown eyes, 'sensible' short blonde hair and a Sloane Ranger accent.

I must have shown my disbelief when she announced she had climbed to 5500 metres and passed a winter survival course in the Scottish Highlands. She promised to prove it and bounced out. Within a day a fax arrived verifying her story.

She hardly drew breath during her trial forced march in the Blue Mountains. Not that she found it tiring, I just couldn't get a word in edgeways.

'I inherited some money,' she told me with disarming honesty, 'so I left England to get away from the protocol, smart parties and the class nonsense. I've been travelling for two years now. My whole life is about having pleasure and being completely hedonistic at all times. The things that give me a thrill in life are basically dangerous, the more dangerous they are the more the adrenalin flows and the bigger the kick I get. I love looking death in the eye and seeing if it will wink back.'

Judging from her conversation she seemed to be mostly interested in two things: mountains and men. I was immediately sold on her. She was a total extrovert, with a quick mind and a great sense of humour. She had all the right experience and I wanted her on the expedition.

Ballantyne was not so sure. 'Trace gives me the feeling that as far as she is concerned no one matters but herself,' he warned.

I did not see it and so I accepted her. She gave up her job at ANZ Travel and took over from Eddie, working full-time on the expedition with me, a move which further soured my relationship with Eddie.

The team had filled out to seven Social Climbers plus Milton. We still had to find two more women, to give us four couples and a butler at dinner.

There were plenty of impressive women in the final ten we interviewed and initially I did not think Sally Guyatt was one of them. But she was very persistent so we agreed to give her a trial bush walk.

She was late. As her new Laser swung into the car park I could hear blaring rap music from inside even with the windows closed. She climbed out looking like she had just come from an all-night party, which she virtually had.

Despite the ill-effects of little sleep, she was classically good-looking with long blonde plaited hair. As we stood watching, she pulled on a pair of Reeboks, pulled herself together and began exerting her considerable charms on us.

Sally worked as a computer analyst and seemed to have an aversion to long-distance endurance sports. The only thing in her favour was she held a brown belt in Tae Kwan Do, a level which I knew required considerable dedication. But she had obviously lost a lot of fitness. As she puffed and panted her way through the thick bush, I began to wonder if she thought she was auditioning as a stand-up comedian. She had an infectious sense of humour and was a compulsive Monty Python and Comedy Company recitalist. I decided she would be perfect if we held the world's highest dinner at the top of Centrepoint Tower and was equally sure that by the end of the forty kilometre walk the comedy routines would be replaced by whingeing and moaning.

Halfway through the hike she tripped and fell face-first into a rock, then sat on the ground, blood streaming from her nose, laughing. I started to change my opinion of her. Anyone who could perform a face plant into a rock and find the experience amusing perhaps belonged on our expedition.

But it was not until the end of the day that she did something that convinced us she was perfect. We had been walking for thirty-five kilometres with heavy packs and we were all stuffed, Sally more than most, when it started to drizzle. On one particularly steep hill she burst out singing the Monty Python classic from *Life of Brian*: 'Always look on the bright side of life'.

We all joined in. It is easy to be amusing and enthusiastic when you are comfortable. We needed people who could be that way when they were totally exhausted.

Not that the media ever thought we were in discomfort. Our press releases conveyed an image of lighthearted fun because that was what the media seemed to crave.

'In preparation for their strenuous ascent, each Social Climber had to sustain an arduous training programme. Each had a two-week crash course in wine-tasting and cordon bleu cooking, while Ballantyne took an exhaustive butler's course at the Regent Hotel. During this stressful period the Social Climbers managed to find time for a spot of croquet for fitness.'

The truth was very different. We had to acquire a lot of mountaineering skills in a short space of time. Our central problem was that Australia has no glaciated mountains. Murf had the impossible task of teaching glacial mountaineering to seven non-mountaineers — without any glaciated mountains.

Each weekend we stayed at his house in the Blue Mountains. We were lowered off cliffs to simulate crevasse rescue techniques and we abseiled through waterfalls as training for descending ice walls. Even Murf admitted they were poor substitutes for the real thing.

In fact the only aspect of high-altitude mountaineering we could come close to recreating at sea level was the 'snow slog'. Forced marches carrying packs filled with twenty-five kilos of rocks, gave a bare indication of the agony ahead. In the comfort of Murf's sitting room he tried to warn us what mountaineering would be like.

'We are trying to achieve something that most people think is impossible,' he gravely informed us, relaxing in an armchair with a can of Foster's in one hand and his baby boy in the other arm.

We sat like giggling school kids not really taking it in, which obviously frustrated him. He took a swig of beer and wiped his moustache dry with the back of his hand.

'There is a chance someone will die,' he said dramatically, trying to make us take heed. 'Youse could be hit by an avalanche or fall in a crevasse. If someone dies the body will be buried on the mountain, I hope youse understand that?'

We accepted this news without a second thought. Talk about death always seems very abstract in our secure society.

'Mountaineering is incredibly uncomfortable,' he continued. 'Once we get to altitude it is terribly debilitating; even thinking is an effort. People's personalities become accentuated. If someone has a bad temper at sea level it gets worse at high altitude. People become unbelievably petty and selfish. We will find sleeping impossible, suffer from thumping altitude headaches and will often be freezing. Walking up the mountain will be unbelievably exhausting, a few grams seem like a kilogram, a metre like a kilometre — you will take twenty steps and collapse.'

We thought he was exaggerating. The idea of taking twenty steps and then collapsing seemed absurd. Neil and I developed a theory on why mountaineers always seemed to overstate the dangers — 'the Everest coffee-shop theory'.

Obviously mountaineering could not be as hard as people

made out, otherwise no one would do it. There had to be rewards at the end of a long climb. We suspected that at the top of the world's highest mountains there were well camouflaged restaurants, climbing shops and modest hotels.

A climbing conspiracy existed. Before a climber could take advantage of these summit facilities they had to swear an oath of secrecy and vow to concoct wild stories about outrageous conditions and mountain dangers. Only then could they plunge into the spa.

The proof of our theory was irrefutable. Why else did expeditions require up to one hundred Sherpas to climb Everest? Obviously, to keep the rest and recreation facilities supplied. Most of them probably carried cappuccino machines, souvenir tea towels and stuffed toy yetis.

No doubt existed in our minds that Murf was a fully paid-up member of this secret high society. He never seemed to have had an easy climb. Avalanches, crevasses and blizzards were the norm. His complicity in the great climbing conspiracy was vital to maintain the tough image of the sport, thereby enhancing its media and sponsorship potential.

This was not a bad thing. Cointreau's decision to sponsor the Social Climbers was worth $66 000 and Ansett Airlines were also interested. I was surprised when Sir Peter Abeles, Chairman of Ansett, agreed to a meeting.

He has a reputation as a tough, overpowering tycoon so I was completely unprepared for his reaction. As I babbled on about the expedition he seemed genuinely amused and interested. Given the normal stresses of his day he may well have found it liberating to chat amiably about dinner parties on top of mountains. Within a few weeks Ansett promised $20 000 on the dual conditions that we take an Ansett flight attendant with us and the world's highest dinner party featured food from the Ansett first class menu.

I was ecstatic. All the expedition costs would now be covered and Neil, Eddie, Trace and I would receive a small wage for all the time we had invested in the project. But sponsorship is a fickle business. Cointreau felt the presence of an Ansett flight attendant would weaken their own exposure and they insisted we reject Ansett's sponsorship.

A month later and barely a month before our departure the whole expedition collapsed. A Cointreau press release was faxed to me, with no covering note and not personalised in any way. It had obviously been sent out to all the media simultaneously. 'Cointreau,' it stated, 'has decided not to proceed with the Social Climbers' project...'

I was stunned. Immediately I tried to contact Colvin Ryan, Cointreau's public relations agency, but no one would talk to me. The receptionist had been instructed to inform me to ring their lawyer. The explanation he gave wasn't satisfactory — to me, at least.

I suspect Cointreau simply got cold feet. Maybe they no longer believed we could make it up Huascaran. Perhaps they feared a death or a PR disaster. Taking them to court was out of the question; we could not afford the legal fees and the case would not be settled before our departure date.

I really believed it was all over. It was extremely doubtful we could attract another sponsor in the short time available and I knew no bank would lend me $66 000. There was only one solution. I went out and bought a lotto ticket.

I felt devastated. Ballantyne did his best to encourage me. 'If it was easy,' he said, 'everyone would do it.'

But for him and Trace I might have given up there and then. She insisted the expedition was not over. Her solution was simple. We would have to trim the expedition expenses down to a minimum, we could not afford an expedition photographer — Milton and I would take the photos — all costs in Peru needed to be reduced and each Social Climber would have to pay at least $3 000. When I did the sums, assuming we could lure Ansett back, I still faced a five-figure personal debt.

Neil drafted a persuasive letter to Tom Dery at Ansett and Tom agreed to reinstate their original offer. Five female Ansett flight attendants volunteered to come on the expedition and the top rating Channel Nine television programme 'A Current Affair' decided to film the selection trials.

On the day of the filming a six o'clock start was scheduled. Murf described what it was like trying to organise us.

> By eight o'clock everybody was still packing the wrong equipment and trying to work out which way was up. Neil was probably on the phone checking the stock market, Avril was two hours late and Sally took a wrong turn and ended up halfway to Lithgow. I began to wonder if we would ever make it to the mountain. Everybody will probably get lost in Lima and end up on a beach in Rio de Janeiro.

Eventually we met up with the 'A Current Affair' team and the flight attendants at the bottom of a canyon in the Blue Mountains. None of them could possibly have been prepared for Murf. He looked worse than normal. Unshaven and wearing a torn wetsuit, which left little to the imagination, he was a fierce sight. He introduced himself as Murf the Torturous Bastard, and proceeded to live up to his reputation. The way Murf saw it, the trials were a triumph.

> We had a great day. We had them swimming in freezing water, doing push-ups in mud and abseiling down waterfalls. Then we slipped a couple of rocks in their packs and made them run up cliffs. At the end of the day of the five original girls, one gave up and one other was obviously a few snags short of a barbie.

The trial was inconclusive. For the first time our ranks were split between three hopefuls. Ballantyne suggested that since the girls would be living with whoever was chosen, the decision should be left to them. They chose Deirdre Rawlings. When I broke the news to her, she claimed to be excited but looked apprehensive, as if she wondered what she had let herself in for.

Deirdre had long plaited light-brown hair and was by far the fittest of the Ansett candidates. She had an air of tough confidence and was obviously bright. I could see she was very determined by the way she approached each trial. She also had the ability to focus herself on the specific task at hand. All of these qualities seemed to make her the right choice for the expedition. However, she did have one weakness. Neil and I suspected she was a loner. During the trial day she had kept to herself and made little effort to get to know either us or the other Ansett women. This worried me because we needed team players.

Deirdre joined the expedition only a couple of weeks before we were due to leave for Peru. Judging by what she wrote in her diary she did not appreciate what she was letting herself in for.

> I applied to go on the expedition, because it sounded challenging and like it was going to be a lot of fun.

With the benefit of hindsight, fun is not a word I would use in connection with mountaineering. Deirdre began to get a taste of what was in store when she was put through a two-day crash course in mountaineering skills by Murf. He then assigned Trace to ensure Deirdre bought all the right high-altitude gear from Mountain Equipment.

Trace now played a central role in the expedition organisation, which always ran much smoother with her around. We often worked until ten at night. After we finished I would fill my pack with twenty-five kilos of telephone directories and power-walk for an hour around Kings Cross. The prostitutes stared at me night after night. They knew that this tall, skinny man with an enormous pack rushing up and down back streets was not a potential customer, but wondered whether they should ring the police or an ambulance.

One evening Trace and I decided to go for an illegal training walk in the Botanical Gardens. It was a mild night for May. We threw our packs over the spiked fence and walked at high speed around the gardens, laughing and tripping over tree roots.

Trace's minute frame was dwarfed by her massive pack. Like a Walt Disney cartoon, it appeared that her pack had grown skinny legs and come to life. After an hour we stopped to rest under the high statue of Captain Arthur Phillip which stands on top of a four metre column.

I suggested we climb the column and to my surprise she agreed. When I reached the top and offered to help she refused, insisting she do it herself.

We sat on top of the column for three hours talking. In recent weeks we had become close, partly from working together but also because we shared the same goal. I admired her irreverence and independent spirit, and she evidently felt she had met a kindred soul.

> *It was like magic that night in the Botanical Gardens. I find it rare to meet someone who likes that sort of bizarre thing and so does Chris. That is why we get on so well together, we both have a mad streak that we find in each other.'*

A week before we left, the documentary crew requested a confidential interview with me. They had bought the film rights for the expedition on the condition we all co-operated fully with their demands. But I was surprised by their first question, 'Who do you think will make it to the summit of Huascaran?'

I had read that Everest expeditions are structured so that only a few of the many team members ever stand on the summit. Initially I had assumed that all of the Social Climbers would reach the top of Huascaran but over the months I had noticed a few subtle comments from Milton and Murf implying otherwise.

This was the first time I'd been asked outright who I thought my summit favourites were. I was convinced Neil would succeed because he is intensely competitive. Murf was so experienced he could not fail. Trace was driven by a strong desire to sit on the summit after being forced to turn back on her last high mountain. I was confident about Avril, as long as she was happy and had someone to follow.

Ballantyne, at sixty-two, was one of the most motivated. 'The opportunity to climb a mountain of this size,' he explained, 'will never come again in my life.'

I did not know about Eddie. Although he was enormously fit, I felt he could tire of the mountain conditions. I thought Deirdre might give up for similar reasons. She was reserved and not as enthusiastic as the others.

In Sally too, I lacked confidence. Like Deirdre, she had been attracted to the expedition because of the humour, but as the truth about mountaineering emerged she became unsure of herself. Her boyfriend Ned Kelly was an important stay. He was an expedition leader himself and had recently raised $350 000 for children's charities by driving a London taxi from London to Sydney. He kept telling her she could do it.

Sally knew she was the least fit member of the team and was painfully aware that others thought she might not make it.

I'm getting annoyed with trying to prove myself. Glen, from the doco crew gave me the 'three ways to die on a mountain' speech — avalanches, crevasses and altitude. I'm sure he thinks we are all a bunch of loonies.

One friend said he had a dream that I am going to die on the mountain. That freaked me out. He then came around to see me, just in case I never came back. So I've scrawled out a will.

40

I ran through my final list and told the documentary that I thought Eddie, Deirdre and Sally maybe would not make it. I was right about one thing — three people did not make it — but I had picked only one.

The night before we were due to leave we had the final team meeting. I tried to explain that tempers on expeditions get very frayed. On the Round Britain Windsurf expedition there had been a lot of shouting. Halfway round the British coast the skipper resigned and the PR man was thrown off the back of the support boat in the middle of the North Sea. He was left treading water and shouting abuse until we weakened and picked him up.

I naively suggested we institute a complete ban on shouting and brawling for the duration of the expedition. The meeting quickly degenerated into a heated argument about whether shouting should be allowed.

On 28 May 1989 I arrived at the crowded airport to find Murf miserably staring at twenty-four Eskys full of camera equipment, lined up at the Aerolineas Argentinas check-in counter. I assumed he was upset because he had just said goodbye to his wife and child.

'If those Eskys,' he morosely explained, 'were full of beers, rather than bloody camera gear, we could spend the whole time in Peru pissed.'

PERU

5
THEY SHOOT
ENGLISHMEN,
DON'T THEY?

---

*To travel is to discover that everyone
is wrong about other countries.*

Aldous Huxley

We were told the word Lima is Inca for lemon. It's actually Spanish for lime. But lemon is more apt.

The story goes, the Spanish asked the Incas to suggest a good site for a port. The Incas hated the Spanish — who had destroyed their empire, decimated the Inca population, held their Sun King for ransom and finally strangled him — so naturally they suggested Lima. It was the worst possible site and the best possible joke. And that was back in 1535. Living conditions deteriorated over the next 450 years.

Today Lima has two hundred thousand people living in relative luxury and six million crowded into hovels. It never rains so cars don't bother with windscreen wipers. The sea is cold and the land so warm that Lima is engulfed in a depressing fog for eleven months of the year.

Peru was in turmoil when we arrived. Inflation ran at 2770 per cent annually. A virtual civil war was in progress. For almost a decade Maoist guerillas called the Shining Path had waged an armed struggle against the government. More than 17 000 people had been killed since 1980.

Classic guerrilla tactics were employed: car bombings, dynamite attacks, assassination of political opponents. And that's just for starters.

45

Few tourists shared their revolutionary fervour. They stayed away in droves. I had always assumed Lima, in darkest Peru, would be an exotic city. It is not. It is a dump of the highest order. However, as they say in the classics, getting there is half the fun. Or in Lima's case all the fun.

Lima was our major stopover en route to Mt Huascaran, in a journey from Australia made up of thirty-one separate stages, ranging in modes of transport from jumbo jets to donkeys. We had ample opportunity to be killed long before we reached the mountain.

Murf was particularly worried about the thirteen scheduled bus trips. A fortune-teller claimed he would die in a horrific bus crash caused by an incompetent driver disguised as a Pakistani. This seemed highly unlikely in South America but there was no point taking unnecessary risks. Bus drivers wearing kafias were boycotted.

But our initiation to the delights of South America had come thankfully not in Lima but in beautiful Buenos Aires. An immensely likeable city, Buenos Aires has been called the Paris of South America. It has wide boulevards, inviting sidewalk cafes, elegant women and enormous steaks.

On our one and only night in the capital we danced the night away at a glitzy nightclub. It was here I learned for the first time about the dangers ahead.

'Peru is in a civil war, you know,' one businessman casually informed me, playing lazily with an olive in his martini, as he leaned against the bar. 'People are being killed daily by the Shining Path terrorists.'

It was news to me. We were advised to rethink our expedition. Bolivia, he explained, was very pleasant at this time of year.

Our problems began in earnest at the airport the next day. As part of our sponsorship arrangements, Aerolineas Argentinas had agreed not to charge us for excess baggage. But the little man wearing a greasy wig at the check-in counter refused to acknowledge any sponsorship deal

46

existed. He insisted we pay six dollars fifty per kilo excess baggage. And we had 1200 kilos!

He didn't look like the diligent civil-servant type so we offered him a one-hundred-dollar bribe. Amazingly it was refused. Then he announced he would prefer to have dinner with our attractive guide, Lolli. Arguments raged, the merits of various restaurants were discussed and time ticked away. Eventually he realised to delay us further would be as unwise as hanging on to a migraine. Suddenly he was all smiles and we were allowed to board.

I slumped into my plane seat and glanced at an English language newspaper from Lima. One look made me sit bolt upright. 'English Tourist shot in Huaraz!' screamed the headline. Huaraz was our ultimate destination before climbing Huascaran. I decided to keep the news quiet to avoid undue alarm. Then I looked around — everyone was reading the same story in horror.

An English tourist had been dragged from his hotel room late one night by the Shining Path and shot dead in the street. His death graphically brought home the reality of terrorism in a politically unstable country.

I was fully prepared to face the dangers of the mountains. There was a real chance of being killed by an avalanche or crevasse. But there was no way I was going to stay in a town where the locals shot Westerners as publicity stunts.

I decided as soon as we landed in Lima I would tell Milton that we had to fly to Bolivia and find another mountain. Everyone was equally horrified and agreed it was better to take our chances with the drug lords of La Paz rather than risk the wrath of the Maoist Mafia in downtown Huaraz.

Furtively, Neil and I discussed the logistics of uprooting the whole expedition to an unknown mountain in Bolivia, a country even more foreign to us than Peru. There were major problems to overcome.

Milton had arranged for us to climb two separate Peruvian peaks. First Mt Pisco (5752 metres), as a training and acclimatisation exercise in preparation for the main event, Mt Huascaran, 6768 metres. Huascaran is the seventh highest mountain in the world outside the Himalayas and the tallest in Peru. We did not know that there was no Bolivian summit even close in height that could be scaled by total novices.

By now the expedition had grown into an unwieldy twenty-four person group, nine Social Climbers, four documentary crew, nine mountaineering guides and two cooks. The situation was made more complicated by the absence of a clear chain of command. Each of the three sub-groups had its own leader. I was in charge of the Social Climbers and Milton commanded the mountaineers. Mike Dillon, one of Australia's most celebrated adventure cameramen whose film credits included Tim Macartney-Snape's first Australian assault on Everest, imposed a measure of control over the film crew. The cooks were a law unto themselves.

There was no clear expedition leader because that issue was never discussed. Moreover, communication was not the strong point of Milton, Mike or myself. But secretly, inwardly, we all felt in control. I assumed I was in charge because the expedition was my idea, but lacked confidence because I knew nothing about Peru, mountaineering or documentaries. Milton was convinced he was leader because he was the Andes expert, but knew he was answerable to Mike and me since we had hired him. Mike paid the bills and wanted some recognition. If we were going to move the whole expedition to a new country, who would make that decision?

Mike Dillon would surely be able to deal with a radical change of plan at short notice. Mike's second in charge was Glen Singleman, who doubled as assistant cameraman and expedition doctor, with Chris Hilton as soundman. Both were Antarctic and mountaineering veterans.

Dr Wolfgang Ebert was the fourth and still-absent member of the documentary team. An aristocratic individual, he was a highly respected director with the German TV station ZDF and had bought German broadcast rights to the documentary. He insisted on overseeing the film production and planned to meet us in Lima. But we could easily intercept him on our way to Bolivia. Yet I sensed he might exhibit German *Angst* at our change of plan, especially since a private porter had been arranged to carry his personal gear.

Our porters presented the major problem. High-altitude porters were scarce in the Andes. Over the years Milton had trained a group of Peruvian porters based in Huaraz, and capable of climbing Huascaran. These porters and their donkeys were critical to the success of the expedition.

The high-altitude cooks fell into the same category. Jenny (Milton's wife) was in charge of the food and had trained a Peruvian assistant, Techi, to climb to high altitudes and cook under severe conditions on the mountain.

Our task would have been much easier in Nepal. There is no shortage of Sherpas in Nepal able to carry all of a climber's personal gear, so inexperienced mountaineers seldom shoulder heavy loads. In the Andes the shortage of porters meant we would be forced to carry twenty kilo packs full of our personal gear and dining accessories, leaving only the food and film equipment to the porters.

Fortunately we did have Nepalese support. Tim Macartney-Snape suggested we fly out Sherpa Tenzing on the basis that no mountaineering expedition should be without its own Sherpa. He was not the Tenzing of the Hillary expedition fame but was certainly a famous mountaineer in his own right and had climbed on three Everest expeditions.

We simply had to assume we could find suitable porters

in Bolivia to replace our Peruvian team. Exactly how we were going to finance the cost of this drastic change of location I had no idea.

I made a mental note never to organise another expedition. As soon as I returned to Sydney, I promised myself, I would take up my nice, easy waiter's job at Darling Harbour. Expeditions were too stressful.

We arrived at Lima airport at midnight. By this time we were starting to look like our passport photographs — far too ill to travel. To my surprise Milton met us on our side of customs. He looked his normal ravaged self. His nose was peeling, his company T-shirt was overdue for a wash and I could see a big toe through a hole in his tatty training shoes. Either he had just stepped on a landmine or this was the 'low profile Peruvian uniform' he had boasted about. Ironically he looked so untidy he stuck out like the proverbial sore thumb. But there were more important issues to think about.

I took him aside and told him about the killing.

'I hadn't heard about that,' he said, totally unconcerned. 'When we're in Huaraz I'll find out the whole story.'

'We cannot possibly go to Huaraz!' I protested.

'Look Chris, just don't worry. Put on this badge.'

He left me holding a pathetic tin badge proclaiming 'I love Peru' in Spanish. Did he really think a bunch of psychotic Maoist extremists would spare us because we claimed to love Peru? They loved their country so much they had taken up executing foreigners.

Milton distributed these badges to the whole party. No one said anything. We were all too astonished at this seemingly pitiful gesture for our protection to comment.

Milton told us to make our way through customs and disappeared like Alice through the looking-glass. Next second he was on the far side of customs arguing with officials.

'The secret of Peruvian customs,' he claimed, 'is knowing how to walk through walls.'

He certainly had the system figured out. Milton made a strange sight — nearly a foot taller and broader than any of the neatly uniformed customs men — he argued our case persuasively.

One of the Peruvian officials seemed to take a shine to Eddie and pointed him out. Eddie was blond, good-looking, and a reluctant veteran of unwanted advances from gays in Sydney. Whatever the customs officials were suggesting, Milton remained steadfastly opposed. My heart sank. The ticket clerk at Buenos Aires airport had wanted Lolli. Now the friendly boys from Lima customs fancied Eddie.

Milton broke off negotiations and came over. 'They want to know if you have AIDS, Eddie,' he said.

Eddie was appalled. 'No way.'

'Basically the head guy won't let us through,' Milton explained with a smile, 'unless we hand over your Ansett T-shirt for his kids.'

As graft goes in third world countries this was pretty minor. Eddie removed his T-shirt and Milton disappeared once more.

Almost immediately he returned with two policemen, hired as our bodyguards. They were found loitering in the toilets and were lured to our cause by the scent of greenbacks.

By now we were all too exhausted to dispute Milton's authority, but were reassured by his dexterity in manipulating the system to our advantage. I stopped bothering about going to Bolivia. Milton was the expert, I would have to take his advice. He warned us to be on our guard outside.

'Peru is a country of kleptomaniacs,' he explained gravely. 'They cannot control themselves. They'll steal anything and once they've got it you'll never get it back. Possession is one hundred per cent of the law here. If they have it then it is theirs. Once we go to the other side of customs, assume everybody is trying to steal your bags.

Half of you push the trolleys, the other half stand guard.'

This inspirational pep talk motivated Murf. His ears pricked up and his moustache bristled. Protecting life, limb and property from the rapacious locals sounded suspiciously like a military operation and he had seven years' experience in the commandos.

'Come on you mongrels,' he shouted gleefully. 'OK Watson, you're loading. Do some work for a change. Trace, you can keep guard, give you an opportunity to perve the local boys. Darwin, you ugly bastard, you're loading. The local kids are too smart for you.'

Immediately we left the safety of customs I knew exactly what Milton was talking about. Everybody was watching us, looking for an opportunity to dive in and score a sixteen millimetre film camera or fake Louis XIV dining table.

Despite concerns about petty theft I felt excited. We had at last arrived in South America proper. Buenos Aires didn't count. It was too civilised, too cosmopolitan. The grinding poverty of Lima fitted my image of South America. It was hot, dry and dilapidated.

Driving through a comparatively rich part of the city the full impact of that poverty became apparent. The streets were deserted and lined with shacks in various states of disrepair. Many were only half-completed.

There were few cars at this hour and those we saw had large chunks of bodywork missing. Working exhaust pipes were rare. Lima wasn't dirty like many third world cities, it just seemed to be falling apart at the seams, but at least there was no evidence of terrorism.

We arrived at our luxury hotel. Most of us felt a little guilty after the street scenes we had just witnessed. Hard-hit by jet lag, Deirdre immediately went to bed. Often when there was loading to be done she would disappear. I was increasingly concerned that she had joined the expedition very late and still seemed to be having problems integrating with the group.

52

We unloaded all 1200 kilos of equipment — for the fourth time in twenty-four hours — and staggered to our rooms to catch a couple of hours' sleep before the early morning flight to Cusco. Not since the Spanish conquistadors plundered the region in 1532 had there been an expedition so laden with gear.

6
'MUCHO PENE'
IN MACHU PICCHU

When in Rome do as the Aussies do.

Murf

Cusco was the capital of the greatest ancient culture in the Americas: the Inca Empire. They didn't invent the wheel or the written word. Yet over a period of a few hundred years they built a massive civilisation which was almost as large as the Roman Empire.

In the sixteenth century the Spanish began their reign of terror through South America. Francisco Pizarro, one of history's truly great bastards, had only 170 men, a few cannons, guns and cavalry, yet in his seemingly lunatic quest for gold he destroyed the entire Inca Empire.

Ironically it wasn't military power alone which defeated the Incas. The Spanish introduced European diseases to which they had no immunity. Smallpox, measles and bubonic plague reached epidemic proportions and decimated the Inca population, reducing it from thirty-two million to five million in less than three decades.

Inca architecture fared better than the people and their culture. The superb Inca masonry withstood Spanish efforts to raze Cusco to the ground. Eventually the Spaniards gave up and built their colonial houses on top of the ruins.

Today, Cusco has a strange appearance. Beautiful white

arched villas with elaborate courtyards are built on massive brown rock Inca foundations: a symbolic reminder of colonial oppression over native cultures.

Every Peruvian brochure features photographs of locals going about their daily life wearing traditional costumes. Careful framing and discreet bribes perpetuate this myth. Virtually no man or child in Cusco wears full traditional clothes. They prefer tracksuits or jeans, baseball caps and trainers. Only middle-aged and older women pose for the camera dressed in all sorts of different styles of hats and the famous multicoloured shawls, often with a pudgy-faced baby gazing inquisitively over their shoulder.

Cusco is at a very high altitude. At 3000 metres, it is 800 metres higher than any mountain in Australia and the first place we visited where altitude sickness was a danger.

Mountaineers speak in hushed tones about altitude sickness, as if it is some virus in the mountain air. One moment you feel great and an hour later it seems as if your brain is being crushed by an iron headband.

Altitude sickness is caused by climbing too high, too fast. The symptoms of the disease are pretty disgusting. Fluids seep out of the capillaries in the brain and fill up the cranial cavities. This pressure on your grey matter causes excruciating and debilitating headaches, vomiting and even death. Alternatively, the same process may take place in your lungs, filling the air sacs with fluid. You can actually drown on the top of a mountain.

The recommended height to climb per day is 300 metres above 3000 metres but even this doesn't guarantee immunity. There is only one cure for altitude sickness. Immediate descent. It doesn't matter if it is two in the morning, minus fifteen degrees Celsius and in the middle of a blizzard, you must get down.

One in ten people don't acclimatise to altitude at all. Chances were one of us wouldn't even make it past base camp but there was no way of knowing who that person would be. The test would come at altitude. That fact created tension for everyone who had no experience at altitude. We were therefore slightly nervous as we flew into Cusco. Sally caught the mood in her diary.

The documentary crew were revelling in the fact that someone might step out of the plane and collapse on the runway with altitude sickness. They would lie gasping for air with the crew feverishly filming them. So I cautiously poked my nose out of the plane and took a couple of trial breaths. I was surprised that I was still breathing normally and didn't feel I would pass out.

To an outsider Sally appeared totally relaxed. Always joking, taking the mickey out of mountaineers and babbling on with Neil in a continual stream of pseudo-mountaineering jargon — but it was just a cover for her lack of confidence.

She was a team player, concerned about others, friendly to everyone. Trace and Avril were strong individuals and Sally welded the three of them together into a group. She got on particularly well with Avril. They seemed a strange combination, the witty city professional and the no-nonsense bush toughie. But each had something the other needed. Avril appreciated Sally's sense of humour while Sally drew strength from Avril's cast-iron confidence in approaching dangerous sports. Sally wrote of her fears in her diary.

I get annoyed with Chris and Neil always hyping about how tough it is going to be and how some of us will probably crack on the mountain. I just want to get on with it. Avril totally agrees with me.

I am the least fit and experienced person on the team. We are constantly reminded that mountaineering has one of the highest mortality rates of any sport. There will be dangers from avalanches and crevasses. Why anyone goes near mountains is becoming a total mystery.

Most mountaineers when preparing for altitude, insist on a disciplined high-carbohydrate, low-alcohol diet. Milton encouraged us to get drunk every evening in the dingy, smoky nightclubs and manically dance the salsa, until the wee small hours: a key reason why we chose him as our guide. Murf was the only other mountaineer to advocate this curious acclimatisation programme.

'Beers and pizza are essential before you leave Australia,' he explained. 'Now we are here you should party till your balls drop off. If you're not drinking so much that you feel sick, your body will never know when it is healthy.'

Murf was enormously confident right from the start. He was an expert on mountaineering and expedition group dynamics. There was a tendency for members of the group to scurry around making friends to build up confidence. Murf didn't need that. He drank, shouted and laughed at and with everyone. He treated this period as a holiday while the rest of us viewed it as vital preparation for the coming physical ordeal.

I was never totally convinced Murf and Milton's acclimatisation programme was the best method of preparing for Huascaran. But it certainly welded the group together, and anyway, we were delighted to have found at least one aspect of mountaineering in which we could all excel.

That first night in Cusco we pushed ourselves to the limits of our personal endurance in a ruthless acclimatisation exercise. By early morning Eddie was lying drunk in the corner of a packed disco grinning like a village idiot, while Avril vainly tried to teach our police bodyguards how to rock and roll.

Ballantyne knew all the latest dance steps but had only a limited command of Spanish. Repeatedly rejected by all the local girls he resorted to a friendly hand on their shoulders and a winning showman's smile while he tried to explain his disappointment.

'Mucho pene, mucho pene,' he shouted in their ears.

They burst out laughing, pointing at his trousers. In trying to say 'much pain' he had obviously got the pronunciation wrong. He had told them he had a big penis.

Ballantyne was a walking comedy routine. He couldn't stop himself constantly giving acrobatic displays, juggling odd items and telling corny jokes. Sometimes we laughed with him, sometimes at him. He didn't mind as long as we found him entertaining. Few sixty-year-olds get on as well with people half their age.

He took no hand in the management of the expedition but acted as a father figure to anyone feeling ill or down. He sensed Deirdre's isolation in the group and tried to encourage her. When Wolfgang joined us in Lima he and Ballantyne became close friends.

Wolfgang immediately exerted a strong influence on the documentary. A doctor of philosophy and film director, he was in his early fifties and made an elegant figure with a neatly clipped grey beard and natty dress sense. He always behaved as if he was about to fight a duel or make a Shakespearan speech, adopting statuesque poses while directing the film, his white silk scarf fluttering in the breeze.

Wolfgang had the job we all wanted. He travelled the world filming strange people doing even stranger activities. A bizarre line of work which suited his eccentric personality. It soon became apparent that he had his own strong ideas about the expedition. Obviously, when he had bought the rights to the documentary, he had gained the impression that the expedition's main aim was to educate the world on the finer points of etiquette — by holding a dinner party at 6800 metres. He could not comprehend it was nothing more than a visual joke.

It was his idea to film a tea party at Machu Picchu, supposedly depicting the Social Climbers polishing their etiquette at altitude. It dawned on me that the real motivations behind the dinner party were being lost in the film version.

To get to Machu Picchu you either walk for five days along the mountainous Inca Trail or risk the train. A few years earlier the Shining Path had dynamited the decrepit train en route, killing the American ambassador during his official visit.

We chose the train.

Ever since the Spanish destroyed the Inca Empire there have been stories about the fabulous 'Lost City of the Incas'. Legend has it that vast amounts of gold had been saved from the Spanish and hoarded in this remote city. Three hundred years later in 1911, the American archaeologist, Bingham, stumbled across Machu Picchu. He was convinced he had discovered the Lost City.

To this day the significance of Machu Picchu is still a mystery. Judging by the number of sacrificial altars and high proportion of female skeletons, most of whom died of syphilis, the site must have held deep spiritual significance.

No photograph can do justice to Machu Picchu. Built on the saddle between two small mountains, there is a sheer drop of almost three hundred metres into the valley on either side of the ruins.

There we were, in one of the most important archaeological discoveries of the twentieth century, a place steeped in mystery, and we were holding a tea party!

We were asked to act out a number of ridiculous scenes for the documentary. Ballantyne pretended he had forgotten to bring the milk for the tea party. We ordered him down to the valley floor to milk a llama.

He later reappeared with our milk but slipped and fell out of sight. We all thought he was play-acting but he had fallen one and a half metres. He described what happened in his diary.

As I fell, I remembered thinking that I mustn't break the milk

jug. My chest smashed straight into a rock. All my breath was
knocked out of my body and I wondered if I would ever get up.
Meanwhile everyone was laughing and shouting for me to keep
moving.

He reappeared looking pale and without his normal
chirpy manner but carried on without complaint. A few
days later it was diagnosed he had cracked two ribs — the
first in a long list of expedition injuries.

By the time filming eventually finished we only had half
an hour to explore the ruins, not nearly enough time. Neil,
Trace, Eddie and I decided to stay the night. Eddie recorded
the events on his Walkman.

I went for a walk with Trace. This was the first time I found out
about her weird sexual ideas and her extraordinary performances
swinging from chandeliers. She left me because she thought it
would be a bit kinky wandering through the virgins' sacrificial
temple.

That night Trace and I slipped past the sleeping guard
and into the ruin. We had the ruins to ourselves. We lay
down together on top of one of the temple walls and closed
our eyes. It was the first time I had relaxed for months.

There is no doubt it is a very special place. The mountains loomed on either side of us. I started to imagine the
last remaining Incas fleeing from the Spanish to this
remote outpost, the death throes of a condemned
civilisation.

Next morning Trace and I climbed Hayna Picchu, the
mountain overlooking the ruins. In the early days of the
expedition Trace had seemed reserved. She was used to
travelling the world alone and found the noise of the group
annoying. Initially she spent most of her time with Neil and
me.

We sat on the top of the peak, overlooking Machu Picchu

and surrounded by mountains in every direction and agreed that this was what we had come for.

Trace looked like a girl on a school outing, with neatly brushed blonde hair, a blue and white spotted bandanna around her head, a pressed white T-shirt and skinny brown legs protruding from a pair of multicoloured watermelon patterned shorts.

Now her girlish face became animated as she excitedly recounted stories about mountaineering experiences, travels, practical jokes, her adventures and her men. She had the knack of describing something in a way that was totally involving, so you felt you were there with her. Some stories were exciting, some amusing. Her Sloane Ranger accent constantly changed in pitch and pace, one moment racing along, then slowing and changing octaves, darting into an impersonation of a local, then carrying on as before. She had a love and zest for life which is rare.

As I listened, I began to envy her lifestyle. She did not care about careers or stability and she had no fear of tomorrow. The important thing was to enjoy life today. It was the opposite to everything we are brought up to believe. I found her wild irreverence and strength very attractive.

There was a pause in the conversation.

'I want to see how much you trust me,' I said.

'I trust you a lot Chris,' she answered excitedly, knowing I'd thought of something.

Without explanation, I blindfolded her with my scarf and led her slowly over the uneven rocky surface to the mountain's edge where it plunged 150 metres vertically into the valley below. I told her to keep her eyes closed and removed the blindfold. Changing my grip to hold her hands behind her, I slowly inched her forward to the edge of the cliff until her toes were over the edge, with only her heels touching the rock.

'Don't move your feet,' I whispered.

If her feet had moved forward she would have fallen. I

might have been able to hold her but because her arms were behind her back I would have certainly dislocated both her shoulders. Probably I would have been pulled over with her.

She didn't say a word. I got a good foothold with my trainers and gradually allowed her to lean over the edge. She was so light I was able to let her tilt forward at a forty-five degree angle.

Her hands gripped my wrists so tightly it began to hurt. She wasn't frightened, just excited. I let her hang there for a moment to feel the wind blowing up the cliff. Then I told her to open her eyes.

She screamed in an enormous release of tension.

She saw there was nothing below her except the distant valley floor. Her body relaxed as she leaned over the cliff, loving the thrill. When I pulled her back her cheeks were flushed and her eyes blazed. She wrote of her exhilaration.

> When Chris and I are on our own away from not only the group but all other people, we are at our happiest. We give full rein to our imagination and can spur each other on to greater heights of the bizarre.

That evening we returned to Cusco and a day later reached our final destination, Huaraz, the climbing capital of South America.

7

WELCOME TO HUARAZ

*It doesn't matter what you do as long
as you look good doing it.*

Neil

The people of Huaraz have definitely upset the gods.
Huaraz is situated in a wide valley surrounded by
the second largest mountain range in the world. Every few
years those same mountains destroy the town.

In 1941 a mountain lake breached its banks after a
massive avalanche, causing a flash flood which wiped out
the city centre and killed 5000 people. Exactly the same
thing happened in 1958, drowning another 4000 people.

The *coup de grâce* occurred in 1970. An enormous earthquake measuring seven point eight on the Richter scale
literally peeled off one side of Mt Huascaran, causing bil-
lions of tonnes of rock and ice to thunder down the valley at
speeds approaching 400 kilometres per hour. Almost ninety
per cent of the town was levelled, with 30 000 inhabitants
killed.

The few survivors were attending a funeral on a nearby
hill. They watched in horror as their town, families and
friends died below. I think this is what insurance companies call an 'act of God'. Needless to add no one in Huaraz was
actually insured at the time.

There seemed to be a pattern of natural disasters striking every fifteen years. The last one was in 1970, so Huaraz

was long overdue for another catastrophe. Maybe we were it.

The locals are a fatalistic lot, seemingly resigned to the fact that apocalyptic acts are a normal part of their lives. Very wisely they make little effort to spruce up the town. No point building a Sistine Chapel if no prayer can stop half a mountain from falling on it.

Huaraz is a disappointment after the colonial beauty of Cusco. It looks like a Mexican shanty town. The only redeeming feature lies beyond: a ring of magnificent snow-capped mountains, the largest of which is Mt Huascaran.

Huaraz has one other claim to fame. It is one of the strongholds of the Shining Path. Only a week had passed since the unlucky Englishman had been shot dead, so we had to be careful. Milton wisely decided to leave our police escorts in Lima rather than risk attracting the terrorists' attention.

The role of bodyguard was taken over by Lorenzo, our head Peruvian guide. Milton told us he was 'connected' with the Shining Path and was therefore our best defence. His logic was lost on me. I thought we were supposed to be avoiding the terrorists, not hiring them.

There was growing concern within the party that a band of Maoist extremists may not appreciate our dinner-party joke. Perhaps they would see it as a serious affront and decide we were the perfect target to publicise their struggle.

I imagined photos published in newspapers around the world. A table laid out with all its finery on the summit. The Social Climbers dressed to the nines around that table. All dead, all slumped face down in bowls of frozen soup, peppered with bullet holes. The English tabloids would have a field day:

Mass murder by Maoist maniacs!
Dinner went off with a bang!
The trout was definitely off.

Milton took no notice of our paranoia and briefed Lorenzo and his porters on the expedition. To our relief they were greatly amused. Peruvians have a great sense of humour and they understood the joke better than many people back home. They thought a dinner on top of the highest mountain in their world was the craziest and most entertaining of gringo schemes.

The truly baffling thing to them was why a bunch of Westerners would travel halfway around the world to climb a mountain in the first place. Nothing grows on snow-covered mountains. They are cold and very dangerous. Peruvians basically believe mountains are places to avoid. The more I thought about it, the more I tended to agree.

We found it amusing that the first mountain we were going to climb was named after Peru's most lethal alcoholic drink — the Pisco Sour, a disgusting concoction which was the cornerstone of our acclimatisation training.

There is an unlikely story that the first people to climb Mt Pisco did so under the influence of this vicious cocktail. As they stood triumphantly on the summit — no doubt nursing terrible hangovers — they decided to name the peak after the cause of their affliction. We felt it was in the spirit of the expedition to tackle this monument to the influence of alcohol.

Apart from the name there were three other very good reasons to hold a dinner party on Mt Pisco. First, it was good high-altitude acclimatisation. Second, even if we failed to climb Mt Huascaran then at least we could claim one successful dinner. Third, Mt Pisco was supposed to be the easiest 5000 metre mountain in the area. Milton had described it as a straightforward seven-day climb. We succeeded in turning it into a fourteen-day epic.

On the day we left for Mt Pisco we met at the climbers' café for breakfast. Most mountaineers had been frightened away to Nepal by the terrorists, so we were welcomed with open arms by the French proprietor.

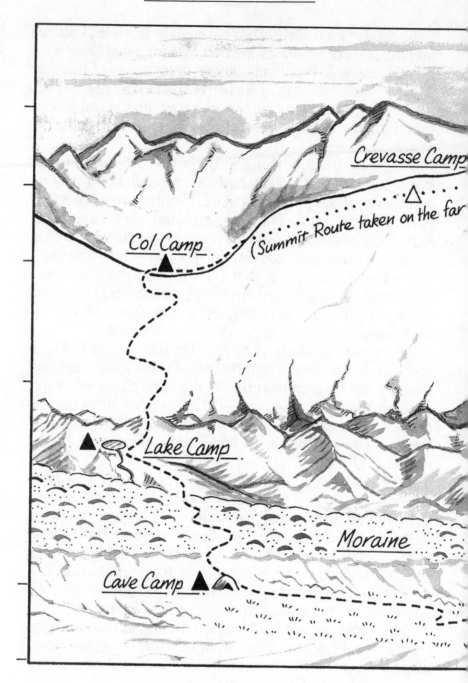

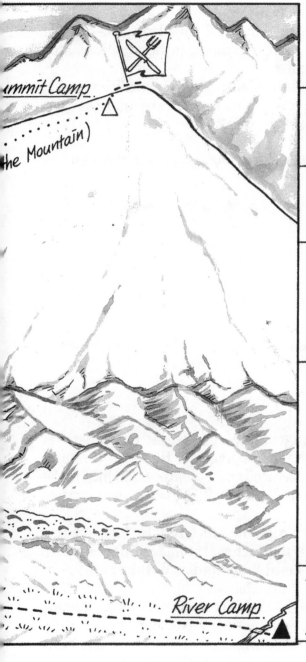

ummit Camp

he Mountain)

Pisco Summit 5,752 m.

Crevasse C. 5,500 m.

Col Camp 5,300 m.

Snowline 5,000 m.

Cave Camp 4,300 m.

River Camp

River Camp 4,000 m.

The café looked like a Swiss coffee shop with massive wooden tables and attractive wood-panelled walls covered with photos of local guides standing in heroic poses atop various Andean summits.

We all felt it was vital to agree on an expedition motto before we left for the mountain. There were many suggestions but no unanimous decision:

It doesn't matter what you do as long as you look good doing it.
Neil

It doesn't matter what you look like, as long as you do it.
Myself

Ignorance is bliss.
Sally

If it was easy everyone would do it.
Ballantyne

More beers, bigger women.
Murf

More beers, bigger men.
Trace

Murf appeared dangerously subdued at breakfast, far from his normal loud and abusive self. He sat at the table pushing a banana crêpe around his plate. Suddenly he let out an enormous burp. The smell of rotten eggs wafted across the table.

'Oh shit, I've got giardia,' he muttered. He looked pale.

Giardia is a debilitating bacterial stomach infection with rotten egg burps as the first symptom. Within an hour he was violently and uncontrollably ill.

I had always thought of Murf as almost superhuman, above disease, altitude sickness or any other mountaineering obstacle. It was a sobering sight to see him loaded into the back of the open-topped beer truck, sick as a dog.

After four flights, thirteen bus trips, two train trips and ten taxi rides we had covered over 18 000 kilometres in seven days. One last dash in the back of our beer truck would finally get us to the starting line for the expedition.

MOUNT PISCO

8
A SHORT WALK
IN THE ANDES

*It's only a couple of hours' easy walk
to the next camp.*

Milton

W e left the valley and climbed up into the Andean
foothills. The bridges spanning the mountain tor-
rents became progressively more rickety. Some bridges
were no more than a couple of enormous wooden planks
held together by metal struts to maintain their correct
width. At each suspect crossing we all had to jump off to
lighten the truck.

Every crossing was filmed in the vain hope a bridge
would collapse. At least they would have spectacular footage of our expedition being washed away.

For the first time we all wore our mountain uniform:
Reebok trainers, navy-blue Peter Storm thermals, red
fluffy jackets and packs. We resembled climbing clones
except for a great variety of garish boxer shorts worn over
our thermals. Modesty dictated that boxer shorts were
essential because thermals have no zips.

We arrived at our drop-off point at 4000 metres just
before dark. We portered our mountain of gear half a
kilometre through a dark wood down to the River Camp.
Eddie recorded the scene.

Like a Trojan, I did five loads while the Poms did bugger all. Neil was just running around telling us all how wonderful it was and how he'd always wanted to climb mountains.

Suddenly I developed an excruciating headache. Altitude sickness had got me. I collapsed into my tent, requesting a cup of tea and a bucket. I never drank the tea but by two in the morning the bucket was in full use. I was throwing up and shitting myself silly, it wasn't pretty. Then the sulphur burps started, like farting through your mouth. Christ, now I've got giardia as well!

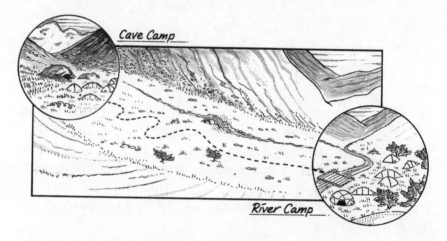

The truck had long gone so there was no way to take Eddie down to alleviate the effects of altitude. He would need to walk ten miles to lose height. Sick as he was, his condition was still mild, so he would just have to stick it out.

Techi produced one of the few good meals on the expedition before we headed for our tents. I have always enjoyed the outdoors but had not camped for years and Neil was nearly as inexperienced. We weren't even capable of erecting the tent. Eventually Tenzing showed us the technique. The thin air at high altitude made sleep difficult, so we talked into the night.

Charisma is an over-used word but Neil certainly has it. He was a vital motivator for the expedition. During the truck trip he had orchestrated group singing, turning an uncomfortable four-hour ordeal into a noisy four-hour ordeal. He perched on the truck cab, wearing John Lennon glasses and a top hat with a small toy koala clinging to the brim. He always wore Union Jack shorts, mainly to annoy Murf.

Ballantyne and Neil competed for the attention of the group. It was hardly surprising that they didn't always get on. My own relationship with Neil was also sometimes strained. One moment he was my strongest supporter, the next he would publicly draw attention to my faults. Neil's nickname for me was 'Ugly'.

Like many doctors, Glen Singleman our cameraman, was very perceptive about people. He understood my relationship with Neil.

> Chris has enormous respect for Neil. Chris is gangly and awkward looking, not only physically but also in his behaviour. For Neil to call him 'Ugly' must have been rubbing salt into Chris's own deep psychological wounds. To make it worse Neil is not ugly, awkward or gangly. When Neil teased Chris about being hopeless with women, Chris became hopeless with women.

But Neil teased everyone, always in an amusing though highly public way. He intuitively understood other people's weaknesses and highlighted them for general entertainment. Generally he knew how far he could go with each person but he sometimes overstepped the mark. At times he could seem arrogant, although he did genuinely care about other people. He knew women found him attractive and he loved to flirt, but remained faithful to his girlfriend in Sydney.

As the long night wore on we debated which of the Social Climbers would reach the summit of Huascaran. Eddie obviously would not make it. If he got altitude sickness at 4000 metres he could never climb a 6800 metre peak. It seemed very unfair he should be knocked down on day one,

75

given all the work he had put in over the past year.

Neil and I both assumed we would succeed, I don't know why. When the subject turned to Trace he dropped a bombshell. Of all the women, he casually announced, he liked Trace the most. Had it not been pitch-dark, he would have seen my jaw drop.

At two in the morning I heard a splash and what sounded like swearing. In my dazed state I assumed a llama had tripped over a tent rope. In fact Ballantyne, squatting with his trousers round his ankles, had slipped backwards down a bank into the icy stream.

By first light he had just about thawed out. It was then we could appreciate for the first time the full beauty of River Camp. A small bubbling brook ran through the green meadow near our tents. The valley spanned only a hundred metres and was defined by steep walls, obscuring all the surrounding mountains except for one enormous snow-covered peak, Mt Chacraraju, at the head of the valley, another unpronounceable mountain which glared down at us as we ate our morning porridge.

Milton seemed impervious to the cold morning air. While the rest of us huddled round the fire wearing duvet jackets, he made do with tracksuit trousers and a blue thermal top.

'That's the way to Pisco,' he casually informed us, pointing out a green-sided valley. 'It's only a couple of hours' easy walk to the next camp.'

I was getting wise to Milton's art of understatement.

Just then Peru's answer to TNT transport arrived. Lorenzo and his offsider Britannion, had herded thirty donkeys up the valley during the night. The film crew sensed this was local colour and jumped into action. Neil 'I love the camera' Watson also sensed an audience and jumped on a donkey.

'I've found a new recruit,' he shouted as he careered around camp. 'He isn't as ugly as Chris. The girls may like him more as well.'

76

Wolfgang intervened. He had gradually taken over the film direction from Mike — and we had to stick to our contract and co-operate with Wolfgang's ideas. For the benefit of the documentary, he wanted to pretend that Neil and I planned to climb the mountain by donkey, each holding three antique chairs.

Like the proposed film sequence, the chairs were fake. I had always wanted the dinner party to look spectacular, but I had discovered the full complement of authentic Louis XIV chairs, mahogany table, silver candelabras, crockery and cutlery would weigh over two hundred kilos. It was impossible to carry such a load up Huascaran without an excessive number of porters.

I had therefore approached two special effects companies in Sydney, Design Field and Local Vertical. They created moulds from the genuine articles and used ultra-light carbon fibre and foam to produce identical replicas, weighing a total of only sixty-seven kilos.

I only remembered how fragile the replicas were as I sat precariously on my donkey, clutching three carbon-fibre chairs. Unknown to me Wolfgang had instructed Milton to belt my donkey on the rump. The poor animal bolted and I was thrown to the ground. A hard landing and an unnecessary trick (Photo 28).

I managed a weak smile as the camera was shoved in my face but inwardly I was furious. I could easily have smashed a chair or been badly hurt. The inventory of illness and injury was already worrying: Eddie, Chris Hilton (our sound recordist), and Jenny (Milton's wife) all had altitude sickness. Milton decided to stay down and look after the incapacitated while the rest of us made our way up the side valley towards Pisco.

Since arriving in South America we had taken every possible form of transport to avoid walking. All our packs were being carried up by donkey to give us an easy first day. I was last to leave the camp.

It is hard to explain what walking at altitude is like. At sea level you set your own pace. At altitude the rarefied mountain air dictates terms to you. When portering our supplies the night before we had all attributed our shortness of breath to the heavy loads.

Now, setting off at a pace which at sea level I knew I could sustain for hours, I was in for a rude shock. Within forty paces of walking up the steep valley side I was gasping for air. I even felt a bit dizzy and was forced to rest. No matter how deeply I breathed I did not seem able to extract enough oxygen from the thin mountain air.

We had all spent the last three months laughing when mountaineers solemnly warned us how tough it would be. Now the joke was on us.

I remembered Trace describing her mountaineering funeral-march shuffle. I tried walking with the heel of my front foot parallel to the toe of my back foot. At least it was forward progress.

Beyond the brow of the river valley lay an even wider valley. Glaciation had profoundly affected this landscape, as if a billion-tonne bulldozer had scraped down the valley, annihilating everything in its path. River valleys are often 'V' shaped but glaciated valleys are always wide and 'U' shaped. Only twelve thousand years ago the ground I was standing on would have been buried deep beneath the glacier.

Pisco valley was a textbook 'U' shaped valley, about four hundred metres wide. I had expected the scenery to look like Nepal with terraced fields, quaint stone houses and locals chasing squealing pigs with long curved daggers. Apart from a couple of miserable red bark trees the valley consisted of only rocks and long, brown-green grass, within an enormous amphitheatre of towering white mountains.

No wind blew, no insects buzzed, no birds sang. The only sound came from a nearby waterfall and my own heavy breathing.

I watched thirty donkeys, seven donkey-handlers, seven Social Climbers, five Peruvian porters, a three-man camera crew, and three guides slowly snake their way up the left-hand side of the valley. Our donkeys could only carry half the massive expedition load: sixteen full packs, dining furniture, enough film equipment to remake *Ben Hur*, several hundred kilos of food, tens of gallons of fuel and eleven high-altitude tents.

It reminded me of a scene described in *The Ascent of Rum Doodle*, an inspired spoof of the early English Himalayan mountaineering expeditions. The following quote was freely adapted for the documentary:

> *Each Social Climber needed two porters and one porter was needed to carry the food for those two and another two would carry the food for those porters. Their food would be carried by a boy who would carry his own food.*

After an hour of walking I had only covered one kilometre. My knee started hurting but there was nothing abnormal about that. I had damaged it a year before running in Sydney's famous fourteen kilometre City to Surf race wearing a top hat, tails and carrying an antique chair. My knee had never fully recovered.

We had nearly four more weeks of climbing ahead. Yet on day one my knee was already giving up. With every step my left knee felt as if someone was jabbing a pin into the tendon. I began using my ski stocks as crutches. Initially this helped but gradually the pain increased with every step.

I sat down and to my surprise burst into tears. I hadn't cried for years and I couldn't understand why I was doing so now. Not just tears rolling down my face but an uncontrollable, gulping crying. I would like to pretend the pain was excruciating but that was not true. I was crying out of self-pity. After two years of planning I knew it was now highly unlikely I would climb Huascaran. I regretted not

79

having trained harder. Obviously my weekly programme, which consisted mostly of walking around Sydney's red-light district, had been insufficient.

I tried to pull myself together by shouting at myself, hoping that verbal abuse would stem the flow. It worked, but only briefly. After limping another hundred metres I started crying uncontrollably again.

I couldn't understand why I could not stop crying.

We had all been told altitude could accentuate our emotions. I didn't realise at the time that I was suffering this effect of altitude. I felt desperate and the altitude magnified those negative feelings. I was behaving as if I was having a nervous breakdown.

Up ahead I could see Neil and Trace waiting for me. They must have heard me shouting at myself in the quiet mountain air. I didn't mind Neil witnessing my distraught state but was appalled to demonstrate such weakness in front of Trace.

'Your knee?' Neil asked when I caught them up. I nodded. He looked concerned. We had always known this could happen.

Trace was wearing three oversized top hats, tipped back on her head so she could see. Her tent-like blue waterproof jacket overwhelmed her tiny frame. She looked like a mischievous five-year-old girl who had raided her father's wardrobe before running away to join the expedition.

'Trace, you look really silly,' I spluttered, smiling through puffy eyes. She looked as sad as I felt. Trace recorded her feelings in her diary.

> I was appalled by the pain Chris was clearly suffering. I knew how determined he was and wondered how much he would endure to achieve his aim.

We shuffled on up the valley in silence.

Up ahead the documentary crew waited like vultures. They sensed a second fatality. We had been walking now

for three hours and it would soon be dark. I had no choice
but to face them.

'Put your dark glasses on so they won't see your eyes,'
Neil said over his shoulder, as we trudged up. 'I'll put mine
on too. They'll think we've all been crying.'

I laughed. Trace hadn't said a word. I think she was
worried she might say the wrong thing, which is exactly
what she did.

'You might as well enjoy yourself,' she said. 'This might
be the last mountain you climb.'

I swung round and shouted in rage. 'You think I won't
make it. I'll get up this fucking mountain.'

She stopped, shocked by my outburst. I grabbed my ski
stocks and limped off in a huff, barging past Neil. Almost
immediately I was in agony again. I went back and apologised. She hadn't meant it that way.

I managed a brave face as I walked past the cameras.

'We are nearly twice as high as Kosciusko,' I told them.
'Almost as high as Europe's tallest peak. We haven't got to
the snowline yet and I feel terrible.'

We trudged on for another hour. Ahead the tents glowed
like a cluster of orange and green lampshades. It started to
snow and the surrounding mountains disappeared into
cloud. It had taken me five hours to cover six kilometres at
an average speed of just over one kilometre per hour.

I discovered I wasn't the only one suffering when I
arrived at camp. Collectively, the Social Climbers were
afflicted with such a diversity of mountaineering ailments
that our camp could have passed for a ward in Kathmandu
Hospital.

Murf had fully recovered from giardia but now had mild
altitude sickness. Deirdre complained of a knee injury.
Avril insisted her altitude sickness was bearable as long as
she did not talk, walk or eat. Ballantyne could barely laugh,
cough, talk or breathe because of his ribs but could still
juggle. Eddie, we assumed, was still throwing up at River

Camp. Neil was popping Panadols.

The expedition had been knocked flat by a so-called gentle, two-hour walk. Our guides were astounded by this pathetic performance.

It was now snowing very hard. I retreated behind one of several large boulders to get away. I blamed myself for the casualties. In selecting the team, I had traded mountaineering experience for personality. Here I was at 4300 metres with a bunch of incapacitated comedians.

Trace appeared with a cup of hot Milo. She offered to share my tent and look after me. I was stunned. Trace lived for pleasure; she was no Florence Nightingale.

The temperature dropped to minus seven degrees celsius and we retreated to our tent. Huddled together in our sleeping bags for warmth, we kissed. At last, I thought, things would work out between us.

But Trace explained her real motivations in her diary.

> *I shared a tent with Chris. I attempted to be sympathetic while being acutely aware my sympathy would probably be misinterpreted.*

9
WHEN DOES
THE FUN START?

Going across the moraine was the single most unpleasant and life-threatening experience I've ever had.

Deirdre

A night of broken sleep did not improve the health of the expedition. Sally was the only fully fit member and she kept apologising personally to everyone for her good health. Murf offered to kick her in the shins so she could suffer along with everyone else. A rest day was decreed.

This gave Murf the opportunity to carry out a spot check on our personal equipment. We had each been given detailed instructions on what and what not to bring. Most of us had ignored them.

Deirdre was caught hoarding a set of philosophy texts and enough cosmetics to set up a high-altitude beauty parlour. Avril's roll-on deodorant avoided detection. Neil's precious dictaphone did not and was immediately jettisoned.

I was the worst offender with a litany of non-essential items: two books, walkman speakers, cassette tapes, nail clippers, deodorant, a backgammon set, fake beard and condoms.

'What the hell are you planning to do with a pack of twenty condoms?' Murf shouted, waving them in the air, amused by my embarrassment.

'I was told you could pee in them at high altitude,' I

whispered, hoping he might also lower his voice.

Murf clearly didn't believe this explanation, suspecting other intentions. Eddie's arrival in camp saved me from being court-martialled. We were all amazed by his remarkable recovery. We had obviously underestimated his determination. He looked his neat self again, blond hair brushed, climbing equipment in perfect condition. Yet only a few hours later he was violently ill again. That all too familiar smell of vomit and diarrhoea wafted from his tent. He was understandably depressed.

I always assumed I would cruise through this whole thing and now it looks like I'll be stuffed from here on. I'm not the only one suffering. Darwin's knee is an absolute mess. I think a lot of people are aware he cannot make it. Murf is still saying he is not a summit man and if he gets buggered he will give up. Maybe he is setting himself up an excuse for when the time comes.

As dusk approached, the temperature dropped below freezing and it started snowing again. Neil, as resident entertainment officer, collected all the foam sleeping mats and spread them round the floor of the cramped five metre cave. A hurricane lamp was lit and we all crammed in: porters, donkey handlers, guides, cameramen and Social Climbers lay on top of each other.

Neil was in his element. He lead the singing with hits from *Mary Poppins* and *The Sound of Music*. For an encore he sang 'New York, New York', impersonating Frank Sinatra, using an ice axe as a cane. With every chorus he cued the Peruvian porters and donkey handlers who enthusiastically sang 'New York, New York' off-key and then laughed hysterically.

I slipped out of the cave, zipped up my duvet jacket against the swirling snow and went for a short walk up the hill. I sat on a rock overlooking the camp, watching the flurries of snow sweeping across the grey landscape. Now and then I could hear the muffled lyrics of the 'Sexual Life of the Camel' escaping from the cave.

A flash of orange light illuminated the snow flakes as Sally, Avril and Trace pushed back the plastic curtain covering the cave entrance. Using head torches for illumination, I watched them weave their way like fireflies to their tents singing, 'She drives me crazy, Oo, Oo. She drives me crazy Oo, Oo'.

Tomorrow, the danger started. The honeymoon was over.

Next day, in true military style, Murf was packed and walking out of camp before most of us had worked out which way was up. He stopped and took some of my gear to lighten my load, then adjusted his pink boxer shorts, donned a top hat and cleared his nose.

'Condoms, my arse,' he grunted. I watched his squat figure shuffle off at the measured pace I knew he could sustain for hours.

Sally and Avril were next out of camp. Sally being a social creature, stopped to chat. She looked sickeningly well. Her blonde hair was plaited and kept in place by a neatly coiled blue bandanna. Even her toy kangaroo, named 'Bambi' by a confused Peruvian child, looked in great shape hanging from her pack.

During this social chitchat Avril was standing beside Sally but mentally she was miles away. Probably re-enacting some riding sequence from *Snowy River II* or a car chase in *Mad Max II*. She wasn't as concerned about her appearance as the other women. Her blue Ansett cap was back to front and her short black hair poked out haphazardly. Her green boxer shorts were oversized.

Finally Sally and Avril moved off. 'Chris, call home, your igloo is on fire,' Sally joked in parting.

Trace and I were the last to leave the camp. Only Deirdre and Eddie were too ill to move. Heart Break Hill, the first section of the day, was aptly named. Not only steep, it was a

Lake Camp

Moraine

Heart Break Hill

Cave Camp

scree slope covered in small loose rocks. Climbing on it was like walking up a hill of large marbles.

No more than a twenty-minute stroll at sea level, it took Trace and me a full hour to scramble up. I hopped as best I could to save my knee. Trace walked behind carrying a full twenty kilo pack, in stark contrast to my empty one.

At the top of Heart Break Hill I saw why our porters were paid danger money for the next section, the moraine. To my left, Pisco Glacier cascaded off the mountain's west peak and churned past me down the valley. The glacier acted as a conveyor belt. It was covered in a layer of smooth rocks which had tumbled off surrounding mountains, producing a lunar landscape.

Glaciers move only a few metres a year but are constantly opening and closing, bending and twisting. This rocky moraine was very unstable. Nothing grew among the piles of loose rocks. Ballantyne described it as one of the most desolate places he had ever seen.

The moraine was too dangerous for our donkeys to cross, so we were our own beasts of burden. Lorenzo and Britannion were in charge of getting all the food and camera gear up the mountain. They were both skin and bone except for barrel chests housing high altitude lungs. Lorenzo's broad smile revealed a few missing teeth. Britannion was never seen without his Los Angeles Rams football cap.

Most of the Peruvian porters were descended from the Incas and were short, averaging only one point six metres, but incredibly strong. They didn't seem to feel the effects of altitude, portering loads across the moraine on our rest day and carrying two or three more loads today. We christened them 'Hombres Supers', a description that delighted them.

They enjoyed a laugh and a beer. Milton warned us not to put temptation in their path by leaving expensive equipment lying around. My own feeling is that they liked us and would not steal anything provided we did the right thing by them. (A few weeks after the expedition, Milton fired

Lorenzo, Britannion and the cook Techi. His camera, passport and money were stolen from his hotel room the same day.)

Sherpa Tenzing carried more loads across the moraine than anyone. Like the Peruvians, he didn't seem to notice the altitude. Tall by Nepalese standards, you could not choose a better person to take on a mountaineering expedition. He was always smiling, sensitive to the needs of others and willing to help. A long green scarf was usually wrapped about his head and he wore a jade lucky charm around his neck. He spoke English like an Anglo-Indian. Everything was 'jolly good' or 'jolly cold'.

Trace and I still had to cross the moraine. Up ahead I could see a few dots of red and purple as the expedition gingerly weaved its way through the maze of rocks and crevasses. The moraine was about one and a half kilometres wide, with the same distance of steep walking up to Lake Camp. It was going to be a long day.

The moraine was never quiet. Rocks were dislodged by the glacier inching forward underneath, causing small but sometimes dangerous rock falls. The most recent victim had been buried in a rock slide.

Each step had to be tested to determine if it was safe. If it was not secure we caused a small rock slide until we found more stable footing. We often fell over. It was better to fall than fight it and risk twisting an ankle.

There was no path. We picked what looked like the best route between mounds of loose rocks. It was far too dangerous to hop across this unforgiving landscape, so I was forced to use my bad leg. The pain in my knee returned. I sank into a gloomy, irritated mood. Trace gradually moved further ahead, wanting to avoid me. I preferred it that way too. I began to think this dinner-party joke was distinctly unfunny.

After two hours I reached the other side of the moraine. The weather reflected my mood. Black clouds enveloped the mountains and it began to snow. Unreasonably, I swore at Milton. He had claimed it rarely snowed in Peru at this time of year and had been proved wrong three days straight. I put on my waterproof jacket for the first time. The bloody zip didn't work. I sat down in a rage.

I had been unbelievably arrogant. I felt frustrated because instead of leading from the front, I was actually holding up the rear. People had to carry my gear because of my knee. I had not even been thorough enough to check my most important piece of survival equipment, my waterproof jacket.

Neil had his own problems. He dropped his load at Lake Camp and met me on the way down. He looked terrible. His blue waterproof jacket hood covered most of his face, his normal effervescent manner had disappeared. Next day Neil described his condition to the documentary crew.

When I arrived at Lake Camp my head was thumping. Altitude sickness had hit me. I knew I had to lose altitude immediately. It was just like in the books. I felt dizzy, nauseous and not caring if I got down. I struggled to get back across the moraine.

At the top of Heart Break Hill one side of my brain told me to lie down and to sleep. The other side, cautious of the dangers, urged me on. I felt like a schizophrenic. The devil on one shoulder and an angel on the other. In triathlons I was used to my body fooling me but not my brain playing tricks as well.

When I got back to Cave Camp I literally couldn't lift a cup and then I was violently ill. Murf stuffed fluids down me and kept me warm. I didn't even have the energy to return any of his abuse. I lay inert in my sleeping bag, wishing I was on a beach in Australia.

It was dark by the time I trudged into Lake Camp. Everyone except Trace was feeling ill and had retreated to their tents. Sally described her day.

I felt sick crossing the moraine. I could sense the danger as the

89

glacier moved underneath and rocks fell. I thought a rock slide could happen at any second. When I arrived at Lake Camp my headache got worse and I vomited.

I think in a perverse way Sally was relieved to finally fall ill. She found it embarrassing to be the only one not suffering.

The following day dawned warm and sunny for the first time since we had been on the mountain. We crawled out of our tents and lay prostrate on convenient rocks, absorbing the sun's rays. Everyone's hair was greasy, no one had washed for five days. We all stank.

Lake Camp lay beside a small, emerald-green pond beneath snow-capped mountains that towered in every direction. The panorama was breathtaking after the ugliness of the moraine. Pisco East peak was the smallest mountain in the range and our summit objective.

Suddenly there was a roar like a long explosion. It startled us. An avalanche peeled off Pisco West peak to our left and thousands of tonnes of snow and ice tumbled down the slope producing an enormous white cloud. It was over in a few seconds and the roar died to a whisper. It was inconceivable anyone could survive if hit by such destructive force.

The avalanche had started from an overhanging snow ridge. Even my inexperienced eye could pick out similar structures in the surrounding mountains. My original scepticism about mountaineering had no foundation; it was every bit as dangerous and unpleasant as the experts claimed.

Three hundred metres below, Deirdre was coming to terms with another danger, the glacier and moraine. She had seen what had happened to Neil the day before and had been told about people being killed by rock falls. She wrote later:

Going across the moraine was the single most unpleasant and life-threatening experience I've ever had.

Eddie and Chris Hilton tried to encourage her across. Eddie described her fear.

> *Halfway across she started to panic. 'No I can't, I can't, I can't,' she said. Chris took her pack and I put on my granny voice.*
> *'Now dear, remember how much we're enjoying ourselves.'*
> *She laughed. Slowly she became more confident. 'When does the fun start?' she asked.*
> *I didn't have the heart to tell her that from what I'd read the higher you go, the harder it gets.*

By late afternoon the whole expedition had reached Lake Camp. Twice as much gear littered the lake foreshores and there was four times as much noise as before. At sunset we were treated to one of those famous mountain sunsets which feature in glossy mountaineering books.

Most people had auto-focus cameras. I had a manual Nikon, tripod and a bag of lenses. While they snapped away I painstakingly set up each shot, experimenting with various lenses and carefully taking light-meter readings.

My methodical approach was a source of great amusement to Neil, Murf and Trace. They stood on either side, whispering helpful hints.

'OK Ugly, don't forget to take the lens cap off,' Neil instructed. 'Quick, someone hold the sunset! Ugly's got to take another light-meter reading.'

Trace explained the teasing.

> *We have a goal to achieve but because it is so absurd it makes us all laugh, so we spend the whole time taking the piss out of it and out of Darwin.*

Neil, Murf and Trace had formed a powerblock. It was no coincidence that they were also the strongest on the mountain, quick-witted and central to the expedition organisation.

After a few minutes the sun disappeared. They lost interest in their carnival of abuse and led everyone to the next event, the evening feeding frenzy.

I was relieved to be left in peace because now I could concentrate on my photography. Jonathan Chester, Australia's most celebrated mountaineering photographer, had told me the best light always happens after sunset. So I waited by myself on a ridge fifty metres out of camp. Everyone by now was stuffing their faces, oblivious to the spectacular light changes taking place.

I glanced up at Pisco West. It looked like there was a massive fire on the far side of the mountain. Black clouds swirled around the summit and vivid orange shafts of light broke through. Behind me the sky had gone purple, the snow turning a gentle pink.

Slowly the light show faded. I was so absorbed I did not notice the temperature plummet to well below freezing. There was already a thin layer of ice on the lake. The others had long finished their supper and lay tucked in their sleeping bags. I was rewarded by the sight of a new moon rising over Pisco West (Photo 31).

By the time I packed up the camera, the camp was quiet. Only Milton was sitting out in the freezing cold, his tatty green duvet pulled over his head. He was keeping some food warm for me.

'What a sunset,' I said ecstatically.

'I've got so many shots of staggering sunsets I don't take so many photographs any more. But I never get bored with the beauty,' he told me, rubbing his hands to keep them warm.

He kept me company while I ate supper. Although I sometimes found him hard to handle I had always liked him. He was, after all, one of the strongest supporters of the expedition.

Next day Glen was teaching Sally, Avril and Eddie to chew

cocaine leaves. This seemed a remarkable thing for a doctor to do but Glen had spent a lot of time in his student days in South America, absorbing local customs. From old photos we knew he had once looked like a refugee from Woodstock, with long hair and flares. The transformation was amazing. Tall and good-looking, he was now in his thirties and had short dark hair.

His diplomatic nature made him a real asset on the expedition. He had a brain which worked twice as fast as most and he always thought carefully before speaking. But sometimes you could doze off waiting for him to finish a sentence, so slow was his monotonous drawl.

'The leaves contain small amounts of cocaine,' he lugubriously explained. 'The Peruvians have been chewing them for thousands of years so they can work at high altitude without feeling the effects of hunger or cold.'

'It helps take your mind off your headache because it tastes so disgusting,' Sally laughed. And promptly retched to one side.

Like a dental injection, cocaine leaves anaesthetise the mouth for some time. Eddie could not taste or feel anything, his whole mouth went numb. A green scum dribbled down his chin.

'Basically I could climb Pisco on my own today,' he joked.

Today was the first day on the snow for everyone except Deirdre, Jenny (Milton's wife) and me. Deirdre was ill with a headache and would not leave her tent. Jenny was also ill with what was initially diagnosed as altitude sickness and Milton had ordered me to rest my knee.

I watched through my telephoto lens as the expedition wandered up towards the snowline. We had to learn safety techniques for climbing in the snow, as well as transport food and equipment to our higher camp, Col Camp. (A col is a saddle between two mountains.)

By eleven, Deirdre still had not moved from her sleeping bag. She lay in her tent staring at the ceiling, looking

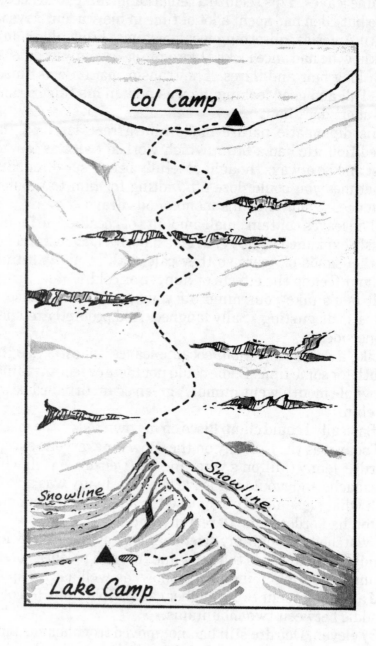

miserable and complaining of a terrible headache. I believed she had a headache, we all had headaches, but I suspected she wasn't that ill. There was no way of knowing. Maybe she had more commonsense than the rest of us. While we laughed off the dangers she was badly shaken by the obvious perils of the moraine and avalanches and dreaded venturing on to the snow. When anyone's back is against the wall they will react in an uncharacteristic way.

Deirdre was not a weak person, in fact she could be very strong-willed. But only a few weeks ago she had casually answered an ad on an Ansett notice board. Before she knew what was happening she was halfway up a mountain in Peru risking her neck.

We had all tried to encourage her, even do most of her work. Murf had warned me that people were getting sick of it and I knew these feelings could lower morale. I was painfully aware I was not pulling my own weight. I did not mind someone dropping out but I could not accept a member holding up the expedition. Both Deirdre and I would have to push ourselves harder.

I decided to call her bluff by telling her unless her headache improved by midday we would have to assume it was altitude sickness and send her down for her own safety. Her reaction was recorded in her diary.

Chris is getting extremely obsessed. The pressure is beginning to show on him, making him unsympathetic and unsupportive, not only to myself but to others.

I feel alone. Chris gave me an ultimatum this morning, either get up or go down. I feel pressured and stressed. I'm missing not bathing, lack of privacy and sure would like to have some of my friends around. I feel it is everyone for themselves. At the beginning the emphasis was on everyone having fun. Now it is dawning on me that high altitude mountaineering is serious stuff.

Just before twelve Deirdre appeared and announced she felt better.

The rest of the expedition returned to camp late in the afternoon. Everyone was excited about their first day on the snow. Trace and Neil were ecstatic. They sat on a rock together telling everyone they could have made it all the way to the summit that day. Neil put one earplug of his walkman in Trace's ear and the other in his own and turned up the volume. He could have been typecast as a Disney pirate with his red paisley scarf wrapped around his head, deeply tanned skin, brown mischievous eyes and pure white toothpaste smile flashing occasionally at Trace as they both rocked backwards and forwards in time with the music.

News circulated about what I had said to Deirdre. Her cause gained little support except from Eddie, hardly surprising given his own bout of illness and the fact that we no longer got on well since I had dropped him from the expedition organisation in Australia. He was furious.

> *Darwin has stuck his fat head in there and turned Deirdre off. She is sick of everything. If we go up Huascaran she's not there. At the end of Pisco there could be a group discussion and Milton will take those of us who don't want to climb Huascaran and go and climb some other peak without the dining room table and other rubbish.*

The atmosphere was getting strained all round. I was finding it difficult sharing a tent with Trace and was jealous of the close relationship developing between her and Neil. Trace was also aware of the three-way triangle.

> *It is a dangerous path I'm treading, weaving in and out between Chris and Neil. Individually I like them both. I am a pleasure seeker on holiday, out for max joy for max time and for a while I was scoring pretty high. But now, I am not only treading on Chris's toes but tramping on his heart. I wish I wasn't so terrible at communicating in relationships.*

I had to get away from Trace. I decided to go up to the Col

96

the next day and stay there while I knew Trace would be sleeping down at Lake Camp.

In the morning I rose early, packed my gear and set off by myself. As I limped out of camp I was relieved to be leaving the problems of the group behind. At the snowline I changed into mountaineering boots, heavy and inflexible, much like ski boots. We had been taught to attach crampons, a slim metal frame of six spikes, to the soles of the boots. The crampons are designed to give climbers a good grip on the snow and ice.

It was another crisp, beautiful day with not a cloud in the sky. I felt as if I was walking through a Swiss chocolate-box landscape.

Few areas of the world today show no trace of human influence. Even Nepal has been scarred by the ravages of countless trekkers and mountaineers. Many of the more popular Nepalese routes are littered with rubbish and some mountains are dumping grounds for tattered tents, ladders and oxygen bottles.

The Andes are so remote and underdeveloped that they are almost totally unspoilt. The only evidence of human contact was an occasional rock cemented down by Murf's toilet efforts, some footprints marking a path through the snowfield or, here and there, a small yellow hole in the snow indicating the spot where someone had relieved themself.

By now I was at 5000 metres. This section was not steep but the altitude made progress excruciatingly slow. My heavy snow boots felt like lumps of concrete moulded to my feet. Thick snow and the fact I was carrying a twenty kilo pack for the first time made it even harder. After each set of twenty steps I had a break to recover.

I was painfully aware I was walking up a glacier which was moving in the opposite direction at speeds approaching a metre per year. At my pace, I convinced myself even that made a difference.

All these factors: lack of oxygen, heavy boots, thick snow, full pack, bad knee and the onward rush of the glacier, combined to reduce my average speed to a spectacular three-quarters of a kilometre per hour: only marginally faster than the top speed of the common garden snail. Fortunately I was not in a hurry.

Normally mountain views comprise three colours only: blue sky, white snow and brown rock. Today there were reds, purples, yellows, spots, paisleys and stripes dotting the mountain path as the expedition scrambled up behind me.

Wolfgang the Immaculate, carried only a designer day pack with not much room for anything other than a few essentials and his brush and comb. He led his entourage of documentary crew, personal porter and camera-equipment bearers, and not surprisingly was the first to catch me up.

He wanted an on-location interview and stood heroically beside me, his neat white silk scarf still fluttering in the breeze. Carefully he positioned his First World War airman-style goggles around his head, removed a rogue feather which sullied his slate-grey duvet jacket and stroked his aristocratic beard.

The contrast was striking. In my rush to get out of Lake Camp I had pulled my thermal top on inside out and was wearing my 'expedition bastard' cap. The cap had a fake hand flicking a 'V' sign sown to the top. Wolfgang detested this cap, pulled if off and, like a climbing nanny, tidied me up.

'Tell me, Chriz,' he said seriously in his thick German accent, 'is zis kind of social climbing here trying to show ze world ze benefits of eticwet.' He could never pronounce etiquette, which was surprising given how often he used the word.

I was dumbfounded. It seemed he was only interested in

repeatedly asking the same question. Once again I tried to explain it was all an elaborate visual joke. Once more Wolfgang showed no interest in any answer other than the one he wanted. He moved on to his second obsession.

'Is Charles Darwin ze inspiration behind ze expedition? Was the fact you failed your biology exam at school an embarrassment to your family?'

Just then the porters strolled past.

'Hola, Darwil,' they cheerfully yelled, saving me from this silly interview.

'Hombres Supers,' I replied.

I'm sure by now the Peruvians thought we were all completely mad. The expedition had always seemed ludicrous to them. But our astounding level of incompetence surpassed that of any previous expedition on record. Seven of us could not even climb. We fell into rivers or off donkeys. And we were always either singing or vomiting. Every step we took was filmed from five different angles. We consistently turned what was a gentle stroll for them into a climb of epic proportions. They could not wait to see the dinner party.

I limped off in pursuit of the Hombres Supers. I still had another three kilometres to reach the col, which didn't seem to be getting any closer. As the sun gained strength it actually became very hot. I stripped down to a single thermal layer.

Soon the Social Climbers started to overtake me. I was pleased when Deirdre passed — it showed her new resolve. I suspect she was delighted to have proved a point. Maybe I deserved a bit of humiliation.

Eventually everyone left me behind. We had so much equipment, each person had to take several loads up to the next camp. Ballantyne and I were exempt because of our injuries.

Everyone dropped off their loads at the Col Camp and filed past me again. I saw Trace in the distance running down the mountain with her now-empty pack. The idea of anyone running at that altitude made me feel exhausted. I sat down heavily in the snow.

I watched her approaching. As usual she looked very neat. Her purple fluffy jacket was unzipped, her blonde hair bouncing up and down with each stride. She had removed the nose guard from her Bollé sunglasses, just in case she was filmed. She had to look good.

At sea level she was just another Pommy traveller but on the mountains her frail body seemed to swell with confidence. The higher she went, the stronger and more assertive she became, while the rest of us weakened. She was physically and mentally in love with the mountains and I was infatuated with her.

'Come on Darwin, it will be dark soon,' the Goddess at Altitude quipped as she ran by. She had a wicked grin.

I muttered something unpublishable under my breath as I watched her run off down the mountain, small lumps of snow flying off her crampons in the soft afternoon light.

The sun dipped below the ridge. To my surprise the temperature dropped fifteen degrees celsius in as many minutes. It was now well below zero and I once again put on layer after layer of warm clothes.

Finally I reached the col. To my right the glacier fell off the mountain in a wave form towards Lake Camp. Col Camp lay in a gully. Three kilometres behind camp I could see Pisco's summit. Neil, Tenzing and Ballantyne cheered me on as I limped towards camp.

'Come on, Fearless Leader, you can do it!'

It was, of course, a joke. Most of the team had taken three hours to climb to the col, it had taken me six. Neil waited at the col to check the last person had arrived safely. He then set off down towards Lake Camp with Tenzing, shouting his normal fanfares.

'See you, Ugly. Don't forget to take the lens cap off.'

Ballantyne and I would spend the night at Col Camp. We

100

had fifteen minutes before sunset. We made ourselves a cup of Milo, unpacked chairs without legs, set them up on the snow by propping up the back rests with ice axes and slumped down exhausted.

'Ahhhhhh. The end of another day in paradise.'

After sunset we crawled into our tents. Ballantyne was suffering from his cracked ribs. The heavy breathing required at altitude was impossible because he could not take a full breath. He was also becoming obsessed with the idea of climbing the mountain and had a habit of counting the number of steps he took each day. Today he had chalked up 2945.

Neither of us could sleep because of the thin atmosphere, so we talked throughout the night. We agreed to ban all discussion about mountaineering. I listened, fascinated, as he told me his life story.

Born Eddie Ash in 1927 at Corrimal on the New South Wales south coast, Ballantyne was a sickly child. A Chinese herbalist suggested a revolutionary cure for the 1930s — exercise. Like everything else in his life he went at it with a passion, working out regularly in the local gym.

By the age of seventeen he had already broken a NSW weightlifting record. Soon after he found his true calling when he took up acrobatics, at which he demonstrated no natural talent but through remarkable persistence, he ultimately excelled. His first job as an acrobat with a circus in Brisbane fell through at the last moment. Bitterly disappointed, he seriously contemplated working as a miner in Broken Hill before settling on a career as a crocodile hunter in Australia's far north.

Fortunately for the crocs, or more likely for Ballantyne, he was passing through Brisbane on his way north when his original job with the circus again became available. He never fired a shot in anger, he never looked back.

In the world of high entertainment there can have been few acts to equal Ballantyne's. It was quite simply unique.

He could balance on his head while flying on a trapeze, a simple feat for a man of his talents, made difficult by his insistence on simultaneously playing a clarinet with one hand and juggling with the other.

His career took off from there. He learned to ice-skate and perfected a daring ice acrobatic act which included a somersault from the trapeze, leading into a sequence of six flip-flaps across the ice.

Australia could not hold him, the world beckoned. He travelled overseas with an ice show and stayed away for seven years. By the time he returned to Australia he was internationally famous.

Ballantyne became known the world over as the 'Upside-down man from Down Under'. He could play golf, ride a bike and play snooker, all standing on his head. His dare-devil feats included performing headstands on the edge of multistorey buildings in London and throughout Europe, Africa and South America.

His acrobatic career continued until his early fifties, when he was advised by his doctor to get out of show business. He married for the second time, fathered two children and became a goat farmer. It was a short retirement. He was soon lured back to the stage as an actor.

Now at the age of sixty-two, he was stuck on a mountain at 5300 metres.

Listening to his story, I began to understand what drove him. I knew he would not have exaggerated anything because he tended to be modest. He had been famous in his youth but as his body slowed with age, his fame had dimmed. During the expedition he acted like a young man. Even his sometimes naive enthusiasm seemed youthful. He was a grandfather who wanted to prove to himself and others he could still perform like a grandson. That is why he pushed himself so hard and seemed accident prone. As dawn approached it occurred to me that he was the only truly exceptional member of the expedition.

10
ALONE AGAIN, NATURALLY

Pisco is a piece of shit.
It is a walk to the summit.

Milton

'Lake Camp, Lake Camp, this is Col Camp, do you read me? Over.'

Milton was having difficulty raising the party 600 metres below. His radio was quiet, then there was the usual crackle and a strange beep.

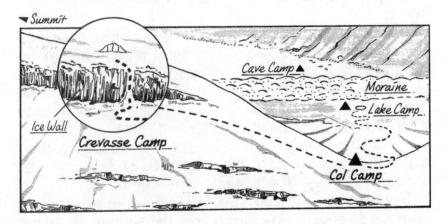

'Hello this is Lake Camp, Mount Pisco.' Neil's voice sounded strangely formal. 'I'm sorry there is no one here to take your call but if you'd like to leave your name and number after the tone we'll call you back as soon as possible. If you are after the Social Climbers they are in Huaraz having a party ... beeeep!'

Most mountaineers would have been scandalised by this frivolous banter. Radio communications, like all aspects of mountaineering, are taken very seriously. But the morning was spectacular, there wasn't a cloud in the sky and the mood of the expedition was high. Milton looked a little dumbfounded by Neil's message so he handed me the radio.

'It is a pity the Social Climbers have gone,' I replied. 'We just heard that the Shining Path have taken over Huaraz. They are looking for any capitalists with arrogant ideas of having dinner parties on their sacred mountains. Please give me a call if any of you survive so I can pay my respects to the dead.'

I wanted to sound as enthusiastic as possible to rally everybody for the climb ahead.

'It is superb up here,' I said. 'It is warm, beautiful weather and the summit looks so close. It would be great to get everybody up to the col today.'

'Roger, understood Bonington, rendezvous at col, over and out.'

Our plan today was for everyone at Lake Camp to climb back to Col Camp and stay overnight. Milton, Jim Nixon (Milton's offsider), and Glen were going to push on to the summit to porter camera equipment. I decided to tag along because Trace would soon arrive at the col and I wanted to avoid her until I had sorted myself out.

Milton had assured us that Pisco was nothing more than a training mountain. 'Pisco is a piece of shit,' he had announced boldly. 'It is a walk to the summit.'

Just getting within striking distance of the summit had been hard enough. Now I could see the summit, at last it looked within reach. Milton and Jim set off and I followed. As soon as I started climbing, I began gasping for breath again. I struggled to get into some rhythm, taking two breaths to each step.

A good forty minutes out of camp, I had only covered 300 metres. Milton was half a kilometre ahead and started shouting down at me.

'Go back to camp and talk to me on the radio,' he bellowed.

I was furious. There I was busting a gut to get up the mountain and Milton insisted I return to camp. Walking 300 metres at that altitude is equivalent to running several kilometres at sea level.

I met Murf coming down the mountain. He had started very early from Lake Camp, struggled past Col Camp, only to be stopped short of the summit by an unexpected obstacle.

'A straightforward walk up Pisco my arse,' he gasped after taking a quick swig of water. 'There's a bloody great crevasse up there ... with a hundred-foot ice wall behind it.'

This was news to everyone. The crevasse certainly did not exist last time Milton climbed Pisco, it had simply opened up and now would have to be overcome.

A crevasse is an enormous gash through the thick layer of ice covering the mountain. Some crevasses are so deep you cannot see the bottom. On the uphill side of the crevasse there is normally a near vertical ice wall. To reach the ice wall without climbing down into the crevasse and up the other side, one must find a natural ramp of snow called a snow bridge spanning the crevasse. Crevasses are dangerous and difficult to cross.

Only Murf and Trace had any experience of them. This could be the moment when those wavering members of the expedition would turn back. I radioed Milton from the camp and he dictated an extensive mountaineering shopping list: four ice picks, three ropes, four ascenders and sundry unpronounceable items of hardware. I did not have a clue how most of them worked or what purpose they served.

'Is it safe?' I cautiously asked him.

'By the time I finish setting up these ropes,' Milton

thundered, 'it will be bloody bomb proof, no worries!'

I loaded all the gear and set off once more. After two hours I was drawing close to the crevasse, but I had only covered a little over a kilometre. I was so exhausted I was hardly moving. The capacity for rational thought had long since disappeared. Instead of using my ice axe for support, as we had been taught to do the day before, I was using my ski stocks like crutches to relieve the pain of my knee.

I traversed across the mountain to reach the waiting party. To my left was a 100 metre steep snow slope leading into a series of crevasses. Milton saw I looked like jelly and came down to help. I was vaguely aware of his concerned expression but could not understand it. He told me repeatedly to use my ice axe but I was so exhausted I ignored him. Milton described what happened next.

> Chris wouldn't listen. He was pretending to ski with ski poles instead of cramponning. Suddenly he slipped and away he went, down into the dangerous sections. I managed to grab him just in time — it was the closest I've ever come to losing a client.

If Milton hadn't been there I would probably have rolled out of control down the slope and into one of the crevasses. I would almost certainly have died. I knew it but was too exhausted to be frightened. I was simply relieved to sit down and rest with Milton's enormous hand gripping the strap in my pack, while Jim rigged a rope so I could safely climb the last thirty metres.

One of Milton's great talents lay in anticipating accidents. There is no doubt he saved several lives and averted numerous cases of frostbite during the expedition. Looking back on it, I now understand why no other mountaineer would touch the Social Climbers.

My fall shook Milton. He told Glen of his concerns.

'Chris is a real worry,' he confided. 'He might push himself to the point of physical damage. I've never seen someone so obsessed, it's clouding his judgment. We'll have to watch him very closely — he's the most dangerous of the Social Climbers by a long shot.'

Milton finally secured all the ropes and worked his way across the crevasse and up the ice wall behind. Glen and I followed.

Climbing an ice wall is a tricky procedure involving an ascender, an ice axe and crampons. An ascender is a ratchet device attached to both the rope and your harness which, because of the direction of its teeth, will only move up the rope and will prevent you from falling.

I teetered my way across a one metre wide natural snow bridge spanning the crevasse. Then I attacked the ice wall. Using the metal spiked crampons on my boots I kicked into the ice, stretched up and swung the ice axe into the wall creating a shower of ice splinters about my head. I then pulled myself up on the ice axe and moved the ascender up the rope to secure myself in case I slipped.

At any altitude this process would be draining. At 5500 metres, it was totally exhausting but exciting. To be honest, anything, literally anything, was stimulating after the monotony of hours of shuffling up the mountain. Milton was obviously relieved that I reached the top without another accident. He knew I was too tired to do any more climbing.

'It's too late to go to the summit today,' he announced. 'You're going to stay here by yourself tonight. We're going back to Col Camp and we'll all join you tomorrow.'

It was pointless to object, he had already erected a tent for me about ten metres uphill from the ice wall. But I was very worried about spending the night alone on the mountain. A barrage of five metre icicles hung from an ice cliff behind me, dripping in the warm afternoon sun. I knew to keep well away. Icicles have been known to drop from great heights and kill people. To my right lay another crevasse. My only escape from these mountain nasties was the path to the summit, running the gauntlet between the crevasse on the left and the icicles on the right.

'Chris, I don't want you to move more than ten feet from the tent, do you understand?'

He had no need to fear on that count, I didn't even *want* to leave the tent. He disappeared over the edge of the ice wall.

I sat at the entrance of my tent waiting for something to happen. Nothing did. I wondered how to kill the eighteen hours until they returned. Pity my backgammon set had been thrown out. The only thing to do was to eat and I could not muster much enthusiasm for my supplies: three litres of water, two tins of tuna, biscuits and chocolate.

After a while I noticed something strange, the total absence of sound. As if someone had suddenly disconnected the sound of a film. No wind, no animal sounds, no voices. In the silence a fart would have sounded like an avalanche.

Gradually, I got used to the quiet. This was truly peaceful. I started to feel more confident and violated Milton's strict rule by walking to the edge of the crevasse. Visibility extended perhaps sixty kilometres over an endless series of snow-capped peaks and alpine valleys. To my right our objective, the summit of Pisco East, lay tantalisingly close. To my left, orange clouds lazily drifted over Pisco West.

I am by nature a cynical person. I had never accepted the spiritual ramblings of committed mountaineers about the mystical power of mountains. At mountaineering slide nights I turned off completely whenever bearded Himalayan veterans droned on about their 'religious experiences' at high altitude.

Yet I knew from recent experience that altitude heightens one's emotions. It had exacerbated my black depression walking up from River Camp on the first day, now it amplified my feelings of peace and contentment. I felt an enormous surge of happiness and an overwhelming sense of wellbeing.

Spending a night alone beneath the summit of Pisco was

a remarkable experience, one of the highlights of the expedition. Sitting on my eagle's perch, overlooking the world, changed the way I view life.

I thought about the problems ruling our lives. Financial worries, career problems and family dramas. I had climbed high enough up the mountain to momentarily gain a clear perspective on such cares. I realised that with the right approach they would all work out and no amount of worrying would make any difference.

Sunset that night was by far the most beautiful sight of my life. As the sun sank behind the Andes, the snow around me changed from orange to pink. The sky on the horizon was like a colour chart. Orange directly above the mountains, merging into red, to pink, through blue to purple. Overhead the blackness of the night accentuated the brilliance of the stars, so close in the thin mountain atmosphere (Photo 30).

The whole scene suggested the hand of God winding the celestial colour chart through a myriad of shades until night fell over the horizon. Throughout this gradual transformation the snow on every peak reflected the colour of the sky, changing from bright orange to red to pink and finally a soft purple.

Hundreds of metres below I could barely make out two people trudging in the snow. They were huddled close together. It had to be Neil and Trace.

'Oiii, Ugly,' I yelled at the top of my voice. They stopped and Neil's reply drifted up to me a few seconds later.

'You're the ugly one.'

These mountains had never before echoed to such sparkling repartee. I stood and waved like a madman, a solitary figure, silhouetted against a luminous purple mountain beneath a starry sky. They waved back but the light was dying and they soon disappeared into the gathering gloom. Now I understood Tracey's intense feelings about mountains.

Mountains are the only places I can be truly happy in. It is just nature, beauty, looking at them and feeling them. They can make me cry with emotion. But it never happens if I'm with someone, even if it is a special person.

It was now completely dark. The temperature had dropped to minus ten degrees Celsius and I had not eaten since breakfast. I wriggled into my sleeping bag and munched half a tin of tuna, some biscuits and chocolate.

My scheduled radio call to Milton was set for nine o'clock. After my near mystical experience in isolation I got mushy and asked to speak to Trace.

'You would have loved it up here Trace.'

In my euphoric state, her two-word reply — 'I know' — said it all.

I bedded down on my solitary outcrop at 5500 metres. The evening had given me a partial understanding of why mountaineers become addicted to these stark, unforgiving wastelands. After virtually no sleep the previous night I drifted into a deep sleep, a feat almost unheard of at that altitude.

11
Toilet Tips
Above the Snowline

*Mountaineering is a series of
alternating extremes, from the
wonderfully awesome to the
horribly awful.*

Trace

A Harvard physiologist studying the effects of altitude looked around the world and saw that 5200 metres is a magic figure. Most human beings die if they stay above this level for extended periods.

At that altitude there is only half the oxygen available at sea level. This means the body struggles to keep going. It gives priority to the brain, vital organs and muscles. Digestion becomes very inefficient and the intestine cannot properly digest proteins or fats, so you start to lose weight rapidly.

If you ever want to be absolutely, positively guaranteed of losing weight, go mountaineering. Eat as much as you like and you will still look like a survivor from an African famine.

Lack of oxygen at high altitude makes it very difficult to concentrate on simple tasks. Packing the tents, rolling sleeping bags, putting on crampons — these and other chores become laborious. It might take forty-five minutes at altitude to achieve what could comfortably be done in fifteen minutes at sea level.

The variation in temperature at high altitude in the Peruvian Andes is astounding. The air is cold but the sun is more intense than in the Sahara Desert because you are nearer the equator and the atmosphere is so thin. Temperatures during the day can vary from well below zero when it is cloudy, up to thirty degrees Celsius in the sun. Yet when the wind comes up it literally blows the heat away.

The risk of serious sunburn is real, even on a cloudy day. You need to keep all parts of your body covered or shaded with maximum sunblock for exposed skin and lips, hats, dark glasses, nose guards and gloves. Even taking these precautions we all lost several layers of skin through peeling.

Serious sunburn may lead to sunstroke. Snow blindness is another danger. The intensity of the sun's rays reflected off the snow can burn the retina causing temporary blindness. Normal sunglasses do not offer sufficient protection but Bollé Irex 100s cut out the harmful rays.

Dehydration is another serious problem above the snowline. Despite the fact that you are surrounded by frozen water twenty-four hours a day, you can never seem to drink enough of it. A number of factors cause this dehydration. The mountain air is dry, the days often hot. Digestion is inefficient so water is not effectively absorbed from the intestine and you suffer from constant diarrhoea.

You must drink five litres of water a day to stay hydrated and you must stay hydrated because dehydration is a contributing factor in frostbite, altitude sickness and exhaustion. This might not seem like a problem on a mountain surrounded by so much snow. But it is a problem. You cannot eat snow because it damages the stomach wall and you could not consume enough to meet your daily requirements for water. So you have to melt it.

The process of making a simple cup of water is a marathon in itself. You need a special high-altitude stove and you need to melt six litres of snow to produce one litre of water. Our three stoves were in constant use to melt enough snow for the hundred litres of water required daily by the expedition.

Altitude affected us all differently. At sea level I could keep pace with Murf on a bushwalk and ride faster on a bike. On the mountain he was incredibly strong and at least twice as fast as me on any climb. Ballantyne and Sally also found the going tougher the higher we went.

Neil and Trace were the strongest performers at altitude yet neither of them escaped its effects. Neil suffered constant headaches and insomnia, while Trace found it hard to sleep because her thin body was especially susceptible to the cold.

Given the appalling conditions on a mountain it is hardly surprising committed mountaineers are an élitist bunch. Unfortunately, some are also a bit sexist and give the impression they consider women and non-mountaineers to be a sub-species. Milton was one of the few mountaineers I met who strongly supported women climbers.

> *Women are put down in society and told they are not as good as*
> *men. But mentally they are very powerful and climbing*
> *mountains is eighty per cent mental and twenty per cent physical.*
> *Women have the mental power to stop physical problems getting*
> *them down. Men don't have that bounce-back capacity.*

In fact we were all pretty sexless on the mountain. The tents were mixed and there was no privacy. Vanity was out of the question: we did not wash or change our clothes for two weeks so collectively we smelt like a farmyard. After a few days our noses stopped registering the stench, making life bearable.

Thankfully our libidos were non-existent. Glen told us the world record for the highest sexual act was at 8000 metres on Everest. A remarkable feat achieved, he said, by a very hard man and a very patient woman. For the average male it is close to physically impossible to get an erection at altitude. Jim Nixon, Milton's offsider, was not an average male, however. On the mountain and in the sleeping bag, he excelled.

Jim's voluptuous Peruvian girlfriend Techi was now the head cook. But melting snow and feeding us took a back seat to her passionate affair with this rugged mountaineer. On every expedition people complain about the food: ours was no exception. The standard of food had deteriorated dramatically when we had left Jenny behind at Lake Camp due to her illness. It was obvious she had been a vital quality control. Breakfast was generally porridge with prunes, and tuna or jam on biscuits for lunch. Dinner was only memorable if Jim and Techi took an early night — Tenzing would then take over and produce a delicious meal — otherwise it was tuna again.

It was important to eat, no matter how unappetising, to keep our strength up. Not that we felt very hungry. But inefficient digestion meant we suffered from constant diarrhoea and farting.

At each camp a crevasse narrow enough to straddle was chosen as the expedition toilet. Visits to the crevasse powder room were vital to monitor dehydration. If your urine was bright yellow you knew you were dehydrating and had immediately to drink at least a litre of water. You tended to feel dehydrated at the end of the day, so you drank more at night. That meant post midnight trips to the toilet in temperatures as low as minus twenty degrees celsius. Up to three times per night.

Peeing was much easier for men than women. In the middle of the night the men could pee into a bottle in their sleeping bags — a good aim was vital — but nature made it impossible for the women. Sally described how unpleasant it could be.

I would lie waiting in my sleeping bag till I nearly burst.
Eventually I could hang on no longer and would struggle out. As I

114

squatted over the crevasse powder room with a minus-twenty-degree-Celsius wind whistling around me, I wondered why I wasn't tucked up in my warm bed in Australia.

On one occasion I forgot the toilet paper but remembered a female mountaineer told me that she always used snow. I tried it to my regret — I think it was a mountaineers' practical joke.

The cold is one of the most unpleasant parts of mountaineering. You sleep in two layers of thermals, a duvet jacket, waterproof jacket and trousers, two pairs of socks, two pairs of gloves, a balaclava and woolly hat, inside a sleeping bag rated for minus-twenty-degree conditions, on an insulated sleeping mat with a foil survival blanket. It is inconceivable that any heat could escape all those layers of high-technology insulation. Yet you still feel the cold. With every breath of frozen air you lose precious body heat.

It isn't surface cold like taking off your dressing gown in a chilly bathroom. It is an aching cold permeating the entire body. The higher you climb the more it seems like a vicious circle. The temperature drops lower, your body uses more energy to keep warm and you burn up more fat. So you feel the cold even more.

At night, water bottles are kept in your sleeping bag with you to stop the water freezing. Socks are pinned to your chest to dry the sweat after a hard day's climb, inner boots likewise sleep with you. If you put on wet socks or inner boots in the morning they may freeze, leading to frostbite.

A strange variety of items were hoarded in our sleeping bags: cameras, film, bottles of wine and champagne. Neil complained of bruising himself on all the equipment after a restless night. Milton even kept a cabbage in his bag which afterwards no one wanted to eat.

Very few people can sleep comfortably above 5200 metres because of the lack of oxygen. As soon as you doze off your breathing slows down, just at the instant when sleep is upon you and your brain suddenly registers a dangerous shortage of oxygen in the blood stream. Sally recorded what it was like.

> *It is a horrid feeling, like someone is gagging you, as you wake up with a jolt, gasping for air. At the high-altitude camps I didn't bother trying to get to sleep. I lay listening to Eddie's breathing and he was doing the same to me. After ten hours the tent would get lighter as dawn approached, then Ballantyne would disturb the peace, shouting at everyone to get up. Another day had started.*

So why do people climb mountains? There is no doubt in my mind that mountains are the most unpleasant environment in the world to visit. Life is brought down to the basics; if you are warm, regular, healthy, not thirsty or hungry, then you are not on a mountain. When you mountaineer you watch your own body fall apart.

If mountaineering can be considered a sport — a matter of some debate — then it is undoubtedly the toughest sport in the world. Tougher even than triathlons or the Tour de France, which are incredible feats of endurance. At the end of the day, competitors in those events get a shower, a good meal and a comfortable bed. Mountaineers can be in discomfort twenty-four hours a day for weeks on end.

Climbing at altitude is a bit like hitting your head against a brick wall — it is great when you stop.

I have asked many mountaineers why they put themselves through such hardships and no one has ever given me a satisfactory explanation. There are however recurring themes: the beauty, the adrenalin fix, the solitude and feeling of oneness with nature, even the prestige. I suspect the simplicity of the challenge is at the heart of it. There are only two possible outcomes: success or failure. If you climb the mountain there is an enormous sense of achievement which spurs you to attempt other peaks. If you fail the frustration can be terrible, which itself drives people to climb other mountains.

No matter how tough it gets there are mountain highs.

116

Certainly we all felt a tremendous sense of euphoria as we neared camp at the end of each day. Partly because of the achievement, partly out of relief but mainly because of the beauty. No photograph could possibly do justice to a mountain sunset at high altitude. Though exhausted, we all experienced a feeling of peace and contentment while sitting in silence with a hot cup of Milo, watching nature's light show. It was Trace who best summed up the love/hate relationship we all had with the mountains.

Mountaineering is a series of alternating extremes, from the wonderfully awesome to the horribly awful.

12
LOST PROPERTY

A fter my night alone, I pulled my sleeping mat out of the tent and left it lying on the snow. A gust of wind caught it and blew it over the edge of the crevasse. I rushed to save it but was too late.

A sleeping mat is not just designed for comfort, it acts as

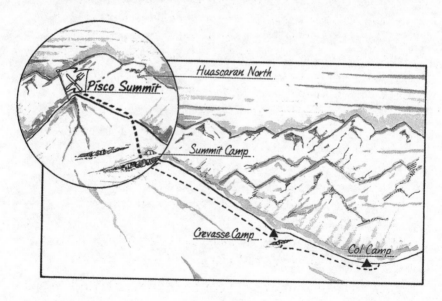

vital insulation between the frozen tent floor and your sleeping bag. I decided to hush up this latest Darwin cock-up — and slip down the ice wall later to check the crevasse.

Soon the silence was broken as the team crossed the crevasse and climbed the ice wall. Neil powered up. I was amazed at the tenacity of Neil and his koala bear — Neil for taking pleasure in this lung-destroying sport, and the toy koala bear for still hanging onto the brim of Neil's top hat. He slumped exhausted at the top of the ice wall.

'That was fantastic... amazing... This is just the best sport,' he gasped.

Murf took over command at the top of the ice wall. Soon there were ropes in every direction, working with military precision. Murf shouted instructions as packs and boxes of provisions were hauled to safety.

This was my opportunity to find my sleeping mat. I clipped on a rope and started down the ice wall. Sally recorded what happened next.

> *Suddenly I saw Chris coming down the ice wall. He looked his normal out-of-control self. Cameras and light meters were hanging in a tangle round his neck, his scarf was about to fall off or trip him up and he was madly flailing around with his ski stocks. He ignored everyone, claiming he was just trying to get some photographs. I had to warn Milton what he was up to.*
>
> *'Jesus, Chris,' Milton shouted. 'Just get back up there. I've told you to stay up. If you don't listen to my instructions you can get off the mountain.'*
>
> *'Ah, er, I just wanted to get some shots ... er ...'*
>
> *'Fucking get back up,' Milton screamed.*
>
> *Chris turned round, looked a bit embarrassed and produced one of his famous platitudes.*
>
> *'Ah, er, good one, um, good one,' he muttered. Then he started climbing back up the ice wall with his tail between his legs.*

I wasn't the only one out of control. As Avril climbed the ice wall, her tent slipped off her pack and tumbled into the crevasse to join my sleeping mat. Unlike me, she seemed unconcerned. Milton must have wondered how he ever came to be involved with such idiots. I was slowly coming to realise that although Milton's job appeared enviable, it was not. Excruciating levels of physical exertion, appalling conditions and the constant stress of trying to prevent any of us from killing ourselves added up to a nightmare profession.

But at least no one seemed to be put off by the climb over the crevasse. We were toughening up both mentally and physically. It was about time.

One by one, we shuffled and gasped the last three kilometres towards Summit Camp, just beneath Pisco's summit. A further thirty metre snow slope had to be negotiated before the dinner party tomorrow.

Avril's lost tent meant I had to share with Milton and Jim that night. Three six-foot-plus men squashed into a two man tent. It promised to be an interesting night. But the real trouble was elsewhere. Avril was sharing with Mike and he was in a bad way. She was very concerned about him.

Mike wouldn't drink all night. He spent the whole time cleaning his camera. He looked a bit strange and very weak.

13
HIGH SOCIETY

---

*Most of ze group don't act like ladies
and gentlemen at all, zey fart
and burp.*

Wolfgang

It was about minus ten degrees Celsius and that was
inside my sleeping bag. I hated to think what it would be
outside. I hadn't slept well as middle man in a two-man
tent, sleeping head to toe. I was vaguely aware that I had
been kicking Milton and Jim in the head all night. It is not a
good idea to keep your mountain guides awake, especially
when your life depends on their alert reactions and clear
thinking.

There seemed to be a pattern on the mountain. Days
started clear and then clouded over. The Social Climbers,
like their urban namesakes, went to bed late and got up late.
We never got started until the sun hit the tents.

I knew from reading mountaineering books that this was
far from the norm. Most other climbers seemed capable of
setting off at ridiculously early hours. Their efforts
inspired me. Foolishly I decided to try an early start, so we
could have our dinner party before the clouds swept in from
the Amazon basin on the east side of the Andes.

'We should all get up before it clouds over,' I suggested to
Milton.

It must have seemed presumptuous to him. He was, after

121

all, the expert. He groaned, sat up and glared at me from the far end of the tent.

Milton never looked sweet-natured at any time of the day but in the morning he looked fiercer than ever. His moth-eaten balaclava covered most of his face. All I could see was a red bulbous nose, which seemed to be permanently peel-ing, and angry eyes. There was something about Milton that always unsettled me. It was not just his enormous build. I knew my uninformed, stubborn behaviour annoyed him. Everyone reaches a point where they lose their temper and I didn't want to be around when it happened to Milton.

'Do you realise you spent most of last night kicking Jim and me in the face?' he growled, giving Jim a knowing glance.

'Sorry,' I said lamely. I was losing the argument already.

'Chris, it is about minus fifteen degrees Celsius. I sug-gest you don't get everyone up. Safety first.' He rolled over and buried his head beneath his sleeping-bag hood again.

I could not believe this was happening. We had worked for years for this and now we were just below the summit of Pisco, no one could be bothered to get out of bed. I ignored his advice.

I put on every layer of clothing I had and crawled out of the tent. There was not a cloud in the sky and it was unbelievably cold. I noticed my feet were torpid and numb but I forced myself to ignore it.

The sun had just risen but would not strike the tents for another hour because we were on the western side of the mountain. I went to seek Neil's support. He unzipped his tent flap, still lying in his sleeping bag, and squinted up to me. He looked like he was nursing a severe hangover.

'Chris, it is too early and too cold, drop it,' he said angrily. Zzipp!

I was shocked. This was the first time he had not supported me. I felt cruelly betrayed. I later found out he had not slept a wink due to headaches and lack of oxygen.

He explained his response to the documentary crew.

> *You must realise that at minus fifteen degrees Celsius, the*
> *incentive to get out of bed to have a dinner party is marginal.*
> *Chris started off as a pretty obsessed and driven character and*
> *became a totally obsessed and driven character, to the extent that*
> *he was almost endangering people's lives. We just stared at this*
> *obsessed bastard.*

Wolfgang and the documentary crew were more encouraging. Glen and Chris had filmed in the Antarctic and thought these conditions were very tame. While we struggled up the mountain they did it comfortably, often walking up and down to film us from all angles. They followed me from tent to tent as I received knock back after knock back.

I realised nothing was going to get people up until the sun hit the tents. I packed the table, a couple of chairs and dining accessories and started the climb up the thirty metre snow slope to the summit. As soon as I was out of camp, Milton countermanded all my efforts to get people motivated.

'Stay in your tents, don't move,' he yelled. 'I'm in charge here, he doesn't know what he is doing. We've got all day.'

Ballantyne was about to follow me up when Milton intercepted him. 'How are your fingers and toes?' he demanded.

Ballantyne was never one to complain. 'My toes are a bit cold,' he admitted, 'but they will warm up once I get going.'

Warning bells rang in Milton's head. 'Oh no they won't! Get back in your tent and get your boots off quickly.'

Once again Milton's instincts were right. Ballantyne was on the verge of getting frostbite. After an hour of massaging and nestling his feet in Milton's armpit, he started to get some feeling back in his toes.

Meanwhile, outside the tents, Murf and Sally were engaged in an obscure dance of dervish origin. Sally's hands were in Murf's armpits, her head completely covered by a red duvet jacket. They waltzed around the camp, stamping their feet, in a kind of hypothermic frenzy. Murf did not hide his annoyance when the cameras rolled on the unchallenged high-altitude ballroom champions.

'Chris is pushing his luck with inexperienced people in this sort of cold,' he said angrily.

Everyone was very wound-up. I looked down from the summit at the camp and could see people were in trouble. Apart from Murf and Sally everyone had retreated to their tents, presumably to allow their feet to thaw out. I was acutely aware that the expedition members were only prepared to follow my bizarre obsession so far.

Then I noticed Neil moving from tent to tent and I immediately became less concerned. I knew he would calm everyone down. He had the ability to smooth the way within the group, one minute joking, the next urging people on. Early in the expedition he had gone out of his way to build up a rapport with everyone, especially the key people — Milton, Murf, Mike and Wolfgang. While I tended to get people's backs up, Neil would follow behind, soothing inflamed egos and resolving problems.

Relieved, I moved back from the edge and sat down. For the first time I really looked around me. The summit was flat, only twelve metres long by six metres wide. The view was staggering. On two sides, the mountain fell away almost vertically. Only a few kilometres away lay the enormous fluted double peaks of Chacraraju, some 500 metres higher than Pisco. It looked like the hull of an upturned boat.

Leading down from the summit ridge, like the ribs of the boat, there were a series of prolonged, near vertical fluted gullies, plunging 2000 metres into the green valley floor. To my left lay the Pyramid of Garcilaso which, not surprisingly, looked like a pyramid. To my right, 1000 metres above me, the north peak of Huascaran towered. Our ulti-

124

mate objective lay behind it, the even higher south peak of Huascaran.

Gazing at Huascaran's vast size I seriously began to question the wisdom of the whole expedition. Maybe we should go for a smaller mountain. My thoughts were distracted by the early morning clouds developing over the Amazon jungle, one hundred kilometres away to the east. They were already pouring into the valley below like an incoming tide. I knew that Pisco would soon be engulfed, shutting out the spectacular view.

Murf was the first to join me on the summit an hour later. I fully expected to cop an earful of abuse but he assured me everyone had calmed down and would be up soon. We started erecting the table. Eddie arrived and still felt I was behaving foolishly.

Chris was typically paranoid. He kept on asking, 'Where are the rest, will we have the party on our own, will we have to take photographs of ourselves?' It was all panic, panic.

The film crew staggered on to the summit carting their mandatory ten camera boxes. Internal bickering was hidden from them and everyone put on their best behaviour. Out came the cameras, on went the show. I dressed in top hat and tails and adopted a plummy accent for the camera.

'We are missing all the girls. I believe they have frostbite.'

Eddie, as usual, looked brushed and clean, his white silk carnation appeared to be genuine and freshly picked. 'Don't worry Chris,' he quipped. 'We'll have a boys' night out, put our feet up, have a few beers and watch the footy on TV.'

Meanwhile Murf was having problems remembering how to lay a table. In stark contrast to Eddie, Murf looked as messy as possible, bow tie crooked and shirt tail untucked, flapping in the wind.

'I must admit I normally eat out of a bowl, with a dirty

125

spoon, sitting on my bum in a tent,' he claimed. 'This is entirely new for me.'

He pulled out his useless electric razor and pretended to shave. 'Since we're going to be the only ones here, I suppose I'd better spruce up my image.' Eddie, Murf and I waited, sitting around the table decked out in all its finery. It was now three hours since I had climbed to the summit and there was still no sign of Neil, Ballantyne and the girls. Unless they arrived soon we would have to have dinner without them, because the Amazon clouds were gaining height on all sides.

Neil was next up, had regained his composure and was his usual ecstatic self. 'This is amazing,' he enthused to the camera. 'I'd recommend it to anyone, at least now I do, although over the last few days I've had my doubts.'

Finally Ballantyne and the women arrived. I apologised for my attempt at an early start. Fortunately the warm summit and stunning views made everyone very forgiving. Avril, Deirdre, Sally and Trace put on their wigs and struggled into thermal balldresses over their mountaineering clothes.

These startling creations were the work of one of Sydney's leading fashion designers, Christopher Essex, his one and only foray into mountaineering wear. A flamboyant individual, he surrounded himself with flashy dames and seemed to smoke incessantly, even though he had lost one lung to cancer. In a fit of gorgeous inspiration he had designed four totally different, equally outrageous dresses.

'Have you ever seen a dream walk?' he cooed, as the girls paraded around his Sydney salon. 'There is absolutely nothing natural in this material. You girls will drive the natives delirious in ... where are you going again?'

Back on the mountain, Sally and Avril finally decided what colour lipstick would not clash — with the scenery, the table-setting or each other — adjusted their wigs to hide their greasy hair and we were ready to begin.

Wolfgang and the documentary crew were concerned that in our moment of triumph we might allow all important standards to drop. He believed there was no point having a dinner party at all if we now abandoned the principles of polite society. So we were expected to enact a pageant, in which we vowed to dedicate our lives to the noble cause of elevating world etiquette.

We had radically different ideas. The whole event was nothing more than an elaborate visual joke. But for the documentary we would have taken a few quick snaps, enjoyed a hurried bite and a chat, and as Murf would put it, 'buggered off down the mountain'.

In truth we were totally unprepared and unscripted. We had been preoccupied with getting to the mountain and then climbing the bloody thing. So we just started casually chatting, blissfully unaware that Wolfgang was in an advanced state of shock. To his horror he suddenly realised he had flown halfway around the world, scaled a 5700 metre mountain and arrived at the wrong dinner party.

To make matters worse his cameraman, Mike Dillon, was seriously ill and barely able to film. Wolfgang rallied his crew and tried to impose order on the proceedings. He decided we must stage an elaborate procession to the dinner table.

We were arranged into a line of couples. Neil with Trace, Eddie with Avril, Murf with Deirdre, and Sally and me. The procession wound its way arm in arm up the mountain, the men taking care not to tread on the girls' dresses with their spiked boots.

We all took our seats. It was a spectacular scene. The table and chairs resembled genuine Louis XIV articles. The trout, silver, china, flowers and glassware created a sumptuous impression, although they were mostly plastic fakes. Even we looked surprisingly clean and smart, despite our nine day ordeal. It was everything I had ever hoped for and more.

127

Despite Wolfgang's concerns, Glen and Chris Hilton were ecstatic about the visuals, an achievement in itself given their normally low-key personalities. Glen doubted it was actually happening.

It was like being in a live surrealist painting. Now I could see what Chris Darwin was on about because it was right there in front of me. It was the most bizarre sight I've ever seen and absolutely hilarious.

The show started. Ballantyne, resplendent in his grey butler's uniform, consulted the menu and recited a tempting litany of courses.

'Entrées today are smoked chicken breasts with mango, or green pea soup with croutons. The main course is delicious, baked lake trout — which I personally caught in Lake Titicaca — served with ginger fronds and accompanied by a macédoine of vegetables and herbed potatoes. For dessert, your choice of cherries jubilee, traditional Aussie damper or fresh fruit.'

It was all nonsense of course. All dishes had been plagiarised from an Ansett in-flight first-class menu. I never saw a cherry jubilee on the whole expedition. In truth, all we had were three smoked trout, carried with us through every stage of the journey from Australia, plus local vegetables.

'Some wine, sir?' Ballantyne asked me.

'Is it room temperature?'

'Yes sir, minus twenty degrees Celsius exactly, sir.'

At that moment two exhausted Argentinian climbers staggered on to the summit: a father teaching his son the joys of mountaineering. Terrorism had frightened most climbers away from Peru, so the mountains were practically deserted. Our dinner-party gatecrashers had not seen a soul during their arduous four-day ascent.

They had climbed the last section expecting to enjoy a quiet summit experience. Imagine their astonishment when they laid eyes on us: a bunch of gringos in top hats, tails and ball dresses, holding a formal dinner party.

Initially, they must have thought they were hallucinating. The combined effects of fatigue, altitude and cold had surely unhinged their minds. They could not have been more surprised if a flying saucer had landed in Buenos Aires. Gradually they accepted that this scene, resembling the social to-do of Melbourne Cup day, was actually happening. They just stood and stared.

Ballantyne hammed it up for the audience. On his rounds serving wine, he fell out of sight with a yell, pretending to disappear into a crevasse. We ignored him; only the Argentinians seemed concerned.

Murf passed on the wine, determined to play the part of the irreverent Aussie to the very end.

'No thanks mate, I prefer a beer. Not a bad drop this local brew,' he explained, opening a tinny which exploded due to low pressure and sprayed him.

Our fish was served. Sally commented that it might be a 'bit high'. We all groaned. No one had time to eat anything because suddenly the Amazon clouds invaded the summit. Within a couple of minutes the sun disappeared, the wind came up and the temperature dropped to well below freezing. We all started to shiver. The mood of the party changed as visibility decreased. We waited in the vain hope the clouds would clear.

Mike Dillon looked dreadful, his face peeling, his lips badly chapped. During the filming Glen had tried to convince him to rest. Now Mike wore a desperate expression, like a man possessed. He sat slumped in the snow. Little did we realise his red blood cells were literally exploding.

Glen realised Mike was at the end of his tether and suggested a cup of tea. An argument broke out when Milton refused to allow it. It started to blizzard and a retreat was sounded.

Everyone grabbed a chair and any salvageable dinner

accessories and disappeared off the peak. Only Neil, Trace and I were left to tidy up. There was no view now, just thick grey clouds streaming over the white summit. It was hard to believe it was the same place I had climbed to six hours earlier.

Despite the weather I was ecstatic that we had achieved our first goal. Already we had set a new altitude-dining record. In a week or so we would attempt to smash it ourselves. In my excitement I hugged Neil.

'We bloody did it,' I yelled above the wind.

'May these be the worst of our days,' he answered, with a warm smile.

It was now snowing hard as we abseiled down to camp. Wisely, everyone was tucked into their sleeping bags except for one solitary figure. Wolfgang was waiting for me, his head hidden under a slate-grey duvet jacket with crimson lining. I could tell by the snow sprinkled on his shoulders that he had waited for some time. He squinted at me through his snow goggles.

As I walked towards him I wondered exactly what I had done to justify such a cold, lonely vigil. I soon found out. Wolfgang was not upset, he was furious.

'I would never have been interested in zis film if I had known it was just about breaking a record,' Wolfgang exploded. 'Most of ze group don't act like ladies and gentlemen at all, zey fart and burp. I had ze impression the dinner would look great.'

I reeled under his assault. The dinner had looked amazing. And anyway, did Wolfgang never break wind?

'The dinner should have been rehearsed. Are we to teach the world a lesson in eticwet because we think eticwet is somezing worthwhile today? You should really teach Murf manners. What you think of American fast food? What is ze importance of eticwet at altitude?'

I did not think etiquette was important at any altitude,

130

least of all on top of a mountain. The only reason we had a butler and served wine from the right was to enhance the visual joke. Debating this ridiculous subject at this altitude in a near blizzard was almost as bizarre as having the dinner party.

'Zere are some people in zis group,' Wolfgang continued without drawing breath, 'who don't belong to ze Oxford University circle!'

I did not have the heart to remind him I hadn't gone to Oxford University; I had gone to lowly Oxford Polytechnic.

'Zere are real Australians. Why don't you teach zem your Oxford eticwets and zey teach you some raw diamond eticwets?'

This sub-zero philosophical tirade took place beside Eddie and Sally's tent. They taped the conversation from their sleeping bags, with Eddie providing a running commentary: 'Bullshit, bullshit. Wolfgang, go home, your igloo is on fire. Whatever you do Chris, don't mention the war.'

I had heard enough. Wolfgang was obviously in the wrong country, on the wrong mountain and at the wrong party. He should have been at a debutantes' coming-out party in Sloane Square or a grand ball in a Prussian castle. As I stared at this obsessed man, it occurred to me that it was he who was the true eccentric and a far more colourful subject for a documentary than we were.

Wolfgang's outburst had attracted an audience, as one by one people wriggled out of their tents into the blizzard to listen. Milton saved the day with a seemingly irrelevant comment.

'I've been bloody annoyed by the lack of involvement of the Peruvians in the film. It is something to do the Oxford thing and that's it.' I suddenly realised Milton was also concerned that we should not be presented as toffee-nosed rich kids playing on the mountain, in case the film damaged his business.

Wolfgang was nearly speechless. First of all the dinner

party had been a bitter disappointment to him, now he thought this huge mountain man had the gall to question his filmic treatment of the porters. He rallied with an equally silly comment.

'I would like to ask ze porters what zey zink about eticwet but I don't speak zeir language.' Now Milton looked confused.

It was a pity Wolfgang never asked the Peruvians what they thought about the expedition. They seemed to have a better understanding than him. He and Milton could have been speaking different languages for all the sense they were making.

Wolfgang's absurd diatribe went on for a full half-hour. By now it was completely dark, extremely cold and totally ridiculous. A debate on etiquette was not worth getting frostbite over.

'I would like to ask ze whole group about zese questions tomorrow,' Wolfgang said and marched to his tent.

Everyone dispersed to the warmth of their sleeping bags. Our camp looked like something from an ice age. The surrounding mountains were engulfed in the driving blizzard. I almost expected a mammoth to lumber out of the darkness and nonchalantly plod past. Maybe that would interest Wolfgang.

I wormed into my sleeping bag between Milton and Jim. Wolfgang had insisted we have another dinner party tomorrow to get it right for his high-brow German audience. But the weather made that look increasingly unlikely.

1. *North Head launch. 'The trick is making it 100% safe but looking lethal.'* Photo: Jonathan Chester (Extreme Images).

2.

3.

5.

6.

2. Avril *Wynne — stunt woman/chicken farmer.*
3. Ballantyne *(Eddie Ash) — acrobat/actor* (Photo: M Sams).
4. Chris Darwin — *waiter.*
5. Deirdre *Rawlings — Ansett flight attendant.*
6. Eddie *Moore — accountant.* Sally *Guyatt — computer analyst.*

7.

8.

10.

9.

12.

11.

7. Murf *(Derek Murphy)* — *mountaineer/ commando/carpenter.*
8. Neil *Watson* — *lawyer.*
9. Trace *Taylor-Young* — *traveller/travel agent.*
10. Mike *Dillon* — *documentary director* (Photo: M Sams).
11. Wolfgang *Ebert* — *German director* (Photo: M Sams).
12. Milton *Sams* — *head guide.*

13.

14.

15.

16.

17.

18.

20.

21.

19.

22.

23.

13. Chris *Hilton* — *sound recordist.*
14. Glen *Singleman* — *documentary cameraman.*
15. Jenny — *cook/Milton's wife.*
16. Jim *Nixon* — *guide* (Photo: M Sams).
17. Lorenzo — *head Peruvian porter* (Photo: M Sams)
18. Nicholas *De La Crue* — *guide.*
19. Sebastian *De La Crue* — *guide.*
20. Techi — *cook.*
21. Tenzing — *guide.*
22. Phar Lap — *donkey.*
23. Vo Rogue — *donkey*

Photographers: Chris Darwin — *photos: 2, 5, 6, 7, 15, 22, 23.*
Wayne Stead — *photo: 4.*
Trace Taylor-Young — *photos: 8, 13, 14, 19, 20, 21.*
Neil Watson — *photo: 9.*
Glen Singleman — *photos: 12, 18.*

24.

25.

26.

24. *'The rig was simple, a few pieces of scaffolding and a kilometre of rope in a spaghetti-like configuration.'* Photo: Jonathan Chester (Extreme Images).
25. *'Murf had the impossible task of teaching us glacial mountaineering without any glaciated mountains.' Author climbing the Three Sisters, Blue Mountains.*
Photo: Alison Murphy.
26. *'Holding a tea party in Machu Picchu was almost sacrilegious.'* Photo: CD.

27.

28.

27. '*A fortune-teller claimed Murf would die in a horrific bus crash caused by an incompetent driver disguised as a Pakistani.*' On roof: Neil, Sally, Murf, Avril. Milton leaning out of door. On bonnet: Trace and Eddie. Photo: CD.

28. '*The poor animal bolted and I was thrown to the ground. A hard landing and an unnecessary trick.*' Jim, Neil and myself. Photo: Wolfgang Ebert.

29.

30.

29. *'Ballantyne was the only truly exceptional member of the expedition.' Lake Camp, Mt Pisco.* Photo: CD.

30. *'The sunset that night was by far the most beautiful sight of my life.' Pisco's summit 2kms in background.* Photo: CD.

31.

32.

33.

31. *The new moon rising over Pisco West.* Photo: CD.
32. *Milton climbing the Pisco ice wall.* Unknown photographer.
33. *'I've got so many shots of staggering sunsets but I never get bored with the beauty.' Milton. Pisco Summit Camp.* Photo: M Sams.

34.

35.

36.

34. *'The women were stronger at altitude than the men.' Thermal ball dresses on Pisco. From left: Deirdre, Avril, Sally and Trace.* Photo: M Sams.

35. *'As he watched Neil and Trace walking to the table, he realised he had travelled halfway round the world, scaled a 5700 metre mountain and arrived at the wrong dinner.'* Photo: M Sams.

36. *'Is the wine room temperature?' I asked Ballantyne. 'Yes sir, minus 20°C.'* Photo: M Sams.

(FOLLOWING PAGES) **37.** *'It was like being in a live surrealist painting.' From pink dress clockwise: Sally, Murf, Deirdre (obscured), Neil, Trace, Eddie, Avril (obscured) and Chris.* Photo: M Sams.

37.

38.

39.

38. *'He was dying in front of us.' Trace and Murf below Pisco's ice wall during the emergency evacuation.* Photo: CD.
39. *'It was fairly obvious I was not wanted so I left them.' Walking towards Huascaran.* Photo: CD.

40.

41.

42.

40. *'I've seen Ballantyne turn from a sprightly character to an old man.'*
Photo: CD.
41. *'Trace enjoyed shocking people with her imaginary perversions.'* Photo: CD.
42. *' "Will the fucking film crew just let us get on with it," Sally yelled.'*
Huascaran icefall. Photo: CD.

43.

44.

43. ' "*This is like the Antarctic,*" *Glen screamed cheerfully.*' *Documentary crew on Huascaran's col.* Photo: CD.
44. '*This is amazing... we love it... too much of this is barely enough.*' *Neil.* Photo: CD.

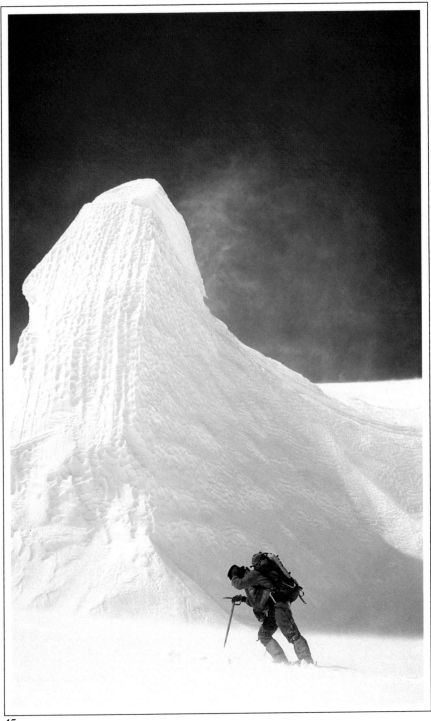

45.

45. *'Neil battling past an ice phallus on Huascaran.'* Photo: CD.

46.

47.

46. *'A dinner party at 6800 metres is impossible, it is like climbing Everest in thongs.' An anonymous mountaineer's prediction.* Photo: M Sams.
47. *'It wasn't a work of art, it was a work of desperation.'* Photo: M Sams.

14
AN EPIC RETREAT

The evacuation was a nightmare. I've never been so scared in all my life.

Milton

As dawn approached the roof of our tent changed from black to green. I had been staring at it for two hours, buried under my sleeping bag. I watched the snowflakes land on the tent roof and slide down the sides like children riding toboggans down a ski slope.

My body had finally had enough. Mountain lethargy had set in and I felt like an old man. I no longer cared about stupid dinner parties or philosophy discussions. I was happy to watch the snowflakes.

After some time I had a gnawing feeling something was wrong. I couldn't work out what it was but the feeling nagged at me. Suddenly I realised. We had not eaten any food at the dinner because it had been cut short by the blizzard. Therefore we had not technically had a dinner party. *The Guinness Book of Records* had stipulated we had actually to eat something for the record to be valid. In my mind we had no choice now, we had to have another dinner on Pisco.

This revelation dramatically changed my mood — I moved. I rolled over and looked out of the tent. Wolfgang was standing in the blizzard listlessly, gazing at the plume of snow being blown off the summit by fifty-kilometre-per-hour winds. For the first time he looked dishevelled. Exhaustion had got to him as well.

I put on my boots and shared a cup of tea with him. The aggression of the previous night had disappeared.

'Maybe zis will clear?' he muttered hopefully, shrugging his shoulders. I didn't answer. We both knew it wouldn't.

'Okay, Chris,' Milton shouted from inside the tent, 'let's have a meeting of the top brass and decide tactics.'

All seven members of the so-called 'top brass' met in Mike's tent. Milton represented the guides, donkeys and the rest of Peru. Wolfgang, Mike, Glen and Chris Hilton represented the combined German/Australian film industries and discerning television viewers worldwide, while Murf and I were mere spokesmen for the Social Climbers.

The situation was perfectly simple.

First, the blizzard was not going to stop that day, it might stop tomorrow, it might not. Second, some members of the documentary team thought we had enough footage on Pisco, some didn't. Point three, we could not be listed in *The Guinness Book of Records*, unless we lied. Points four, five, six and seven: everyone was exhausted, some wanted to stay on the mountain, some wanted to return to Huaraz, some wanted to head home to Australia. Eight, we were running out of food and fuel and nobody quite knew how long our supplies would last. Factor nine, we could not leave the mountain until we had tidied up, but that meant sitting out the blizzard. Which brought us back to point one.

Finally, we were running out of time. We should have been half-way up Huascaran by now. Milton had originally allowed twenty-three days to climb Huascaran. There were only fifteen days left.

Given all these variables, rational decision-making would have been difficult at sea level. In our high altitude daze we completely lost the plot. The debate became highly-charged, very personal and overly emotional.

Milton was not on good terms with the doco crew because of the argument about Mike's cup of tea on the summit. Chris repeatedly asked him how long it would take to climb Huascaran. Milton seemed incapable of giving a straight answer and I didn't blame him. After all it had taken us eleven days to climb what should have been an easy seven-day mountain and it was not over yet. Milton got progressively more angry as Chris's cross-questioning continued. The tent was already stretched to capacity. I was convinced that at any moment a fight would start, the tent would rip and seven grown men would spill out on to the snow like a tag-team wrestling match.

Reaching a consensus on any single issue was impossible. Wolfgang insisted we have another dinner on Pisco so he could conduct summit interviews. Chris, Glen and Murf thought we should evacuate Pisco immediately and start climbing Huascaran to give us a fighting chance to 'bag it'.

Milton obviously thought our performance on Pisco was so disappointing we didn't have a hope of climbing Huascaran. He felt we might as well re-climb Pisco to obtain better footage.

I was shell-shocked by this change of heart. He knew Huascaran was the expedition goal; he was the one who had proposed it. I hinted to Milton that if he wouldn't take us up Huascaran I would find a guide who would. I could see him balancing the pros and cons of continuing to lead this inexperienced group. If he continued against his better judgment and someone became badly injured it would severely damage his career. If he refused and we succeeded on Huascaran with another guide, that would also damage his reputation. He had to weigh up whether we were more determined than dangerous.

Mike hardly said a word. His health was steadily deteriorating the higher we climbed. His boyish face was peeling badly and his lips were so chapped they were swollen. He lay in his sleeping bag, surrounded by his beloved camera equipment. When asked his opinion he whispered that we should abandon both Pisco and Huascaran and return to the Inca capital Cusco to film more local colour! With hindsight, I now realise he wasn't thinking straight, he was dying.

I was the last to express my views and I did not mince words. If we went straight to Huascaran and failed we would have no world record since the dinner on Pisco was invalid. We had to have a second dinner on Pisco and there was no question of not climbing Huascaran afterwards, with or without Milton, the film crew or anyone else.

The debate raged for two hours with no agreement. A decision had to be made and Milton lost his patience and made it.

'We are going down,' he ordered, 'stocking up with food and re-climbing this mountain, if only to tidy it up properly. If you want to have a dinner party, that's your business.'

The meeting was over, thank God.

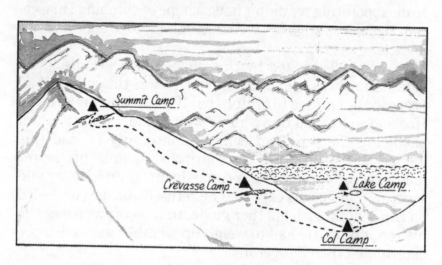

No one was happy about re-climbing Pisco. We had all had enough. Everyone was dirty, hungry and exhausted. Milton's primary concern now was Mike's health. He appeared to have severe altitude sickness and had to descend immediately. Milton described the situation.

Mike was in deep shit without gumboots. A few more red blood cells exploded in him, he was becoming delirious. I was petrified. I told him to get ready for an immediate evacuation.

There was a desperate panic around camp as everyone packed their gear. Lorenzo warned Milton that Mike was refusing to move from his tent. Every warning bell, siren, alarm, klaxon, gong, tuning fork, fog horn and xylophone sounded in Milton's head. He swayed momentarily under the cerebral uproar.

'Bloody bullshit,' he roared. 'Mike is leaving this instant.'

When Milton lost his temper only a madman would stand in his way. He stormed over to Mike's tent and ripped it open. 'Right, we are going, buddy,' he ordered.

Mike turned over, his eyes half-shut, 'Let me stay, I'll be all right,' he slurred.

'No, you're going down now, even if I have to carry you.' Milton dragged him out of his bag and forced him to put on his boots. He described his feeling of desperation.

The evacuation was a nightmare. I've never been so scared in all my life. Mike was dying in front of me and the weather was deteriorating.

We all roped up and started down, as fast as we could safely go. Tenzing walked in step beside Mike. Every time Mike collapsed, Tenzing would catch him, lie him in the snow, massage his legs, lift him up and get him going again. Eventually we reached the crevasse. Milton recalled the crossing.

We rigged Mike on an abseil rope. He was lying down like a pile of shit and we abseiled down with him. When Mike was at the bottom I shouted to Tenzing, who is super strong, to get him the hell out of there and to the safety of Lake Camp. It was one of the scariest situations I've been in. It wasn't within the safety margins.

It was dark by the time I reached Lake Camp. All the tents were full except the hospital tent with Mike Dillon. I opened the flap and was hit by a vile stench. None of us had washed for eleven days but our noses no longer registered the smell of each other's body odour. The stench in Mike's tent was not the smell of giardia or vomit. It was a new smell, heavy, repellent and putrid. It smelt like rotting flesh. I had read about the smell of death and this is how I imagined it. Mike was snoring, so at least I knew he was still alive.

A metre away in the next tent Ballantyne lay awake. He too was suffering.

The pain in my ribs was so bad I was fighting for every breath. I was worried I would fall asleep and die. I just lay awake all night trying not to move, staring at the roof of the tent, waiting for the dawn. It was the worst night of my life.

15
ONCE MORE
WITH FEELING

I kept looking behind me and saw Trace
powering to beat me to the summit.
I wasn't going to let her do that.

Deirdre

Milton, Jim, Tenzing and Lorenzo left for Huaraz early the next day to buy more food and fuel for the second assault. Mike was too ill to go with them but the experts expected him to recover soon from his diagnosed altitude sickness, now that he was at a lower height. For the rest of us it was like a day at the beach. All the sleeping mats were laid out and everyone relaxed in the warm sun.

Wolfgang gathered us together. He wanted to ask, one final time, why we were here. He was once more a vision of sartorial and manicured splendour, his beard neatly trimmed, his hair immaculate.

'Zis seems to be a satire of ze formal parties that take place all over ze world that have no meaning at all, just outside appearances,' he postulated.

There was a silence as we tried to come to terms with his new theory. He had discarded his bizarre notion about etiquette in favour of an equally dubious proposition. He looked hopefully at us, we stared blankly back.

'Wolfgang, you are trying to make us into characters we are not,' I said. 'It is beginning to annoy us. Normally we treat Ballantyne as a friend but we are being forced into treating him like some lowly servant. The way you are

139

presenting the film, the audience will think that is our normal behaviour.'

We were concerned about what would end up on the screen. Any documentary is only an interpretation of events, but this was verging on fiction. The real us could easily finish up on the cutting room floor, replaced by images of chinless Hooray Henrys and shallow Sloane Rangers.

No one minded that Wolfgang droned on all morning. Since we all enjoyed the sound of our own voices, we enjoyed correcting him. He put forward every possible explanation for the dinner party. We rejected them all. By the end he looked disheartened.

I felt a bit sorry for him. Essentially he was a genuine man, dedicated to his job, which was to produce the best possible entertainment. We were probably a disappointment to him, our expedition had not lived up to his philosophical expectations.

After the meeting we spent the afternoon lying in the sun. Everyone had their individual sense of humour which came to the fore whenever the pressure was off. We chatted happily, enjoying the break and each other's company.

Ballantyne was the only one not joining in. Whenever I spoke to him a smile flashed across his face but it was not genuine. At his age, the hardships of the last eleven days had hit him harder than most. His normal smiling face was now gaunt, his silver hair was heavily matted and the veins in his legs were very obvious. He had lost his youthful enthusiasm and optimism, stopped being the entertainer and was in a lot of discomfort. He kept his pain well hidden but confided in his diary.

Each time I breathe there is a click as the ribs rub on each other. It's very painful. I've also run out of Zantac for my ulcer, which isn't making life any better.

I could see he did not want to climb Pisco again but I knew he would never admit it. So I suggested he stay at Lake Camp to look after Mike and build up strength for Huascaran. He was obviously relieved.

No one could doubt his determination. His body had lost most of its fat and was now eating away at the muscles. I started to doubt his chances on Huascaran. Willpower alone could not overcome a frail body.

Milton, Jim and Tenzing arrived back in camp early next morning, having walked through the night. I could not believe my eyes when Milton proudly unpacked our high-altitude supplies which included cornflakes. Somehow I never imagined Chris Bonington living on cornflakes on Everest.

Lorenzo had disappeared during the return journey. Apparently he had got blind drunk in Huaraz and had fallen asleep in a ditch. When Milton woke him, he screamed and ran away in panic, leaving his pack behind. He reappeared two days later looking sheepish.

He missed the turning point of the expedition. In one day we reclimbed from Lake Camp to the Summit Camp, where previously it had taken four days. Over the last two weeks our bodies had acclimatised to altitude, desperately producing more red blood cells to carry extra oxygen.

During the first climb up Pisco most of us felt as if we were suffocating. This time the difference was startling. It was still as hard as running a marathon but this time we coped a lot better. Everyone, including Milton, realised Huascaran was a possibility.

Milton's theory about women on mountains proved correct. They were carrying the same load as the men, had far less illness and climbed faster. Murf privately admitted that if anyone succeeded on Huascaran, it would be Trace, Sally and Avril. Those three got on very well together and

141

encouraged each other. Trace, being the experienced mountaineer, had taken over the role of Amazon leader from Sally.

Trace enjoyed schooling Sally and Avril in mountaineering but was frustrated when Deirdre ignored her advice. Now that I was not sharing with Trace, she had moved in with Glen and Deirdre but the two women were not getting on well. They were complete opposites. Trace loved the outdoors, living rough with no luxuries, while Deirdre craved a warm bath, a comfortable bed and a little indulgence. Yet Deirdre showed her true form on the second climb up Pisco. She described the race which developed between her and Trace to the summit.

> I felt very comfortable climbing today and took the lead. Every time I looked behind me I saw Trace powering up trying to beat me to the summit. I wasn't going to let her do that!

Deirdre won.

An hour later I arrived exhausted, unaware of the race between Trace and Deirdre. I was surprised and delighted when Trace came and asked me if she could move out of Deirdre and Glen's tent and join me instead. Trace felt the cold more than anyone else and knew I would keep her warm, make her cups of tea and run errands. However, she acknowledged the drawbacks in sharing with me.

> I don't think Chris and I are very tent-compatible. I like to be very orderly, whereas Chris chucks everything everywhere, which upsets my delicate nerves.

The next morning dawned cloudy. But as quickly as the clouds had come in during the first dinner, they lifted for the second. Although Pisco is not a particularly high mountain, it has one of the best views in the Andes. Today was a day to enjoy it. As the early morning sun appeared, the temperature rose ten degrees and we all felt euphoric. All except Murf.

Re-climbing Pisco had been a trial for him because of a continuous hacking cough he had developed. Overnight his cough worsened and he was hit by giardia again. Avril and Neil spent the whole night looking after him. Neil had slept only two nights in the last five.

For filmic continuity Murf had to be at the table. We virtually had to carry him to the summit and change him into his formal wear. He sat impassively in his chair, even his moustache looked limp.

The dinner party started and I made a short speech. I was well aware of Wolfgang's desperate need for me to say something about etiquette. So I obliged.

'One small step for man, one giant leap for culinary etiquette,' was my offering to him. I knew if only one comment finally made it into the documentary it would be that one.

At this dinner we made sure we all ate something, Wolfgang got the footage he wanted and we all became mildly drunk. Alcohol affects you three times more at altitude, so our one bottle of Hardy's Chardonnay gave good value.

We'd done it. I knew the photographs would look fantastic. Even if we failed to climb Huascaran, the expedition would still be a modest success. I did not mind if anyone decided to drop out now. In many ways it made sense to trim the team to a small, highly motivated group and let the waverers waver off.

One by one people drifted back down to camp. I pottered around the summit, tidying up and enjoying the breathtaking view. Neil, Trace and I were the last on the summit. I asked if they were coming down with me.

'We'll be down in a second,' Neil answered casually. I left them. They did not reappear for an hour. Trace described her feelings.

During the dinner, we could have been sitting in the Blue

143

Mountains outside Sydney for all the wonder I felt. The whole touring circus of Social Climbers, film crew, guides and porters completely destroyed the atmosphere.

Neil and I sat on the summit in silence for some time and I felt those beautiful surges of emotion that only mountains inspire in me. It is only in silence and solitude that you can forget your own existence for a moment and open up your mind and your soul to the awesome timelessness and vastness of the universe. These experiences are like a drug for me and I know the mountains are where I can get a shot of it. I will always be addicted.

Neil is one of the most unemotional people I know, which made what he wrote even more extraordinary. Like Trace he was deeply affected by the experience.

I sat at the summit and savoured the solitude, the enormity of the world, the insignificance of man and it didn't seem to matter. I was just one of those few lucky people in the world to enjoy a moment like that. It helped put the other aspects of my life in perspective.

By the time Neil and Trace returned to camp most of the expedition had set off down the mountain. As I packed my rucksack I noticed they seemed strangely aloof from the rest of the group. They did not want to talk to anyone else and were content to be silent in each other's company. Glen was one of the last to leave camp and recorded his thoughts on what was happening.

Chris is becoming like a puppy dog to Trace, wagging his tail whenever she is around. But Trace is quite taken by Neil's sophistication. He's a smooth operator, so much more socially adept and charming than Chris. You've got Neil on one hand and puppy-dog Chris, who is rather embarrassingly making advances towards Trace on the other. She has actually rejected Chris and formed an allegiance with Neil.

Today Trace asked me, in front of Chris, if she could move back in with Deirdre and me again. I agreed. Chris was

144

devastated. She had cut him off at the knees. His face fell on to the snow, he turned round and crawled away.

Deirdre watched with interest. I doubt she cared about what was going on between the three of us but she knew what Trace was doing.

It is becoming apparent to almost everyone that Trace is playing Neil and Chris off against each other. She is acting like a princess and Neil and Chris have to duel for her. I can see it is Neil she has her heart and mind set on so it is quite amusing watching her antics.

16
ICE FALLS
AND BEER STAGGERS

I set off down the mountain. By the time I arrived at the top of the ice wall it was late afternoon. The temperature had slipped to minus four degrees Celsius. Sally was huddled in the snow gully, waiting to cross the crevasse when I slumped down beside her.

Like all good soap operas, everyone in the group knew everyone else's business. Sally was aware of the three-way triangle between Trace, Neil and me. She chatted merrily to cheer me up. She prepared to cross the crevasse, zipped up her red gortex jacket, flashed one of her big grins, pointed her ice axe at me and started singing, 'Always look on the bright side of life'.

She shuffled off to the ice wall, still singing, with her toy kangaroo Bambi bouncing on the back of her pack. As her voice became muted over the edge of the wall, the mountain stillness crept back. The only sound came from the wind gently blowing down the gully. I was sitting where I had camped during my solitary night, and remembered that incredible sunset.

The Andes were wearing different clothes this evening, shrouded by puffy clouds, like Wolfgang's grey duvet jacket. Jim watched Sally abseil safely out of sight. 'Okay

Chris, let's go,' he barked.

Despondently I scraped the ice off my crampons to give myself a better grip on the tricky ice wall and limped over to him. I hated crevasses.

'Milton, Chris is coming down,' Jim bellowed. In other words prepare for a disaster. I attached my ski stocks to my pack and swung around to clip myself on to the abseil rope. In the process I nearly speared Jim's face. Like some Charlie Chaplin skit, he ducked to avoid the metal spikes.

'For Christ's sake, Chris,' he muttered, too tired to be angry, 'be more careful, you nearly had my eye.'

I knew this would only strengthen his conviction I was dangerous. I mumbled my apologies and started to lower myself over the edge, walking backwards down the face towards the crevasse.

As I abseiled down, the tube of plastic flowers attached to my pack slipped out. Praying no one would spot my most recent mistake, I watched them roll down the slope and disappear out of sight. The silence was broken by a shout from below.

'Bloody hell, Darwin, you're a real worry,' Milton roared, as the orchids flew past him and vanished into the crevasse.

It was careless. I could have dropped my ice axe and hit him. I needed both the orchids and the respect of the guides for Huascaran. At the moment I had neither.

Approaching the near-vertical ice wall I glanced over my shoulder and saw Milton glaring up at me. He was standing on the far side of the snow bridge across the crevasse. Bits of ice had been knocked off the snow bridge as each member of the expedition crossed, so now it was only half a metre in width.

I was in trouble. On each side the bridge fell away vertically into the depths of the crevasse. Standing on the snow bridge I relaxed momentarily and peered over the edge.

'Steady Chris, don't look down,' warned Milton.

147

I should have paused to regain my concentration but I rushed to cross the bridge and get to safety. Stepping backwards, my left foot sank into the snow, deeper than I had expected and the weight of my pack pulled me sideways. For a second I was frozen, teetering on my left leg and then, ever so slowly, I started to topple.

I could not see Milton but he echoed my thoughts in the quiet mountain air.

'Oh shit,' he whispered.

As I started to fall it never occurred to me that I would get hurt. I was more worried that this would confirm my accident-prone reputation. Desperately I tried to swing my ice axe into the wall but failed to get a hold. I tumbled out of control down into the crevasse. Gripping the rope for dear life, I swung pendulum-like along the ice wall. At the last moment I managed to twist myself backwards and my pack protected me as I slammed into a row of two metre icicles, giving the insides of the crevasse a neat crewcut.

I hung in the crevasse panting, trying to calm myself. Then lumps of ice started falling on me. Someone did not realise I had fallen in and was climbing down the ice wall above me. I was not wearing a helmet and knew if a piece of ice hit me on the head it could knock me out, causing me to let go of the rope. I started to panic.

'Whoever's fucking climbing down, stop!' I screamed.

As usual Milton demonstrated his vast experience in dealing with beginners. He quickly calmed me down.

'Just stay where you are, Chris. Don't worry. I'll pull you out,' he reassured me. After a few minutes I was relieved to be standing back on terra firma.

Milton could see I was shaken up and tried to bolster my shredded confidence. 'Well done for not letting go of the rope,' he said with a warm smile. It was the only thing I had done right.

Now I had to retrieve the flowers. To my surprise, Milton fully supported my plan to abseil down into the crevasse.

148

Either he took the view that having fallen off the horse I had better climb back on again or perhaps he hoped the crevasse would swallow me up once and for all.

I noticed the strange effects within the crevasse, as the light bounced off each facet of ice. Even stranger, the crevasse resembled the storeroom of a mountaineering shop. Obviously climbers had been dropping equipment into it over a period of months. My sleeping mat, Avril's tent and our plastic flowers all sat on two snow ledges. I could not believe my luck.

I climbed out with my trophies in semi-triumph. Milton smiled at me. He was delighted I had actually done something right for a change. We set off down the mountain towards Lake Camp sounding like a West Indian steel band as the numerous expedition pots and pans clanged together on the back of his pack.

'I bet you'll never go near a mountain again after this,' he joked.

'Oh no, no,' I lied, 'I'm enjoying it.'

Milton and I were like chalk and cheese. The only thing we had in common was that we were both smarter than we appeared. He sometimes seemed bumbling and incoherent but actually made good decisions, even if he was bad at expressing them. Earlier, we got on well because of mutual respect. My respect for him had strengthened but whatever respect he had for me had long since disappeared.

His years of experience told him that with my accident rate it was only a matter of time before I got seriously injured. There is an apt mountaineering motto: 'There are bold mountaineers and old mountaineers but no old, bold mountaineers'. I was one worse than bold, I was careless.

Jenny's health was weighing heavily on Milton's mind. He was concerned that her condition had not improved and knew he had lost a vital member of his team which was making expedition life more difficult.

He soon tired of my snail's pace and lumbered ahead, into

the night. Once again I guarded the expedition's rear.

Two hours later as I neared Lake Camp I heard laughter as Milton recounted his battle to get me safely across the crevasse. Evidently everyone found it hysterical. No one seemed to accept that I was more susceptible to the forces of gravity than most. If today was a fish I would have thrown it back.

Next morning we walked across the moraine to Cave Camp where our donkeys waited. Mike's condition had not improved. His face looked like cracked mud and his lips were now so badly chapped that deep cuts had developed. His body was giving up on him. Both Glen and Milton realised he was suffering from something more serious than altitude sickness alone, but could not decide whether he had hepatitis, malaria or jaundice. Mike was loaded on to a donkey and led down the mountain, where the truck was waiting.

When Neil and I arrived at the beer truck we could not

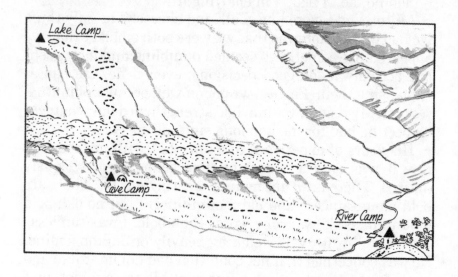

believe our eyes. After two weeks craving for a beer, there was a whole crate of local lager sitting on the road and four female Social Climbers drinking in the truck cab.

Within half an hour Neil and I had polished off four large bottles of beer. We lay sprawled on the road, listening to Elton John, watching the lake in the valley turn orange with the sunset.

Over the past fortnight we had all been under considerable stress. For the moment it was over and we all felt an enormous release of tension. In the truck cab the women were obviously more drunk than we.

'More beers, bigger men. More beers, bigger men,' Trace chanted out of the window, hitting the truck with her palm in rhythm.

The two drivers were very encouraged by Trace's motto. It was not every day they had four admittedly smelly but none the less very attractive Western girls shouting for men. One of them was particularly keen on Sally. In broken English he kept inviting her out to a disco and lecherously asking her the name of her kangaroo.

'I don't know,' she muttered, 'Bambi or something.'

He grinned, showing his rotten teeth and mumbled, 'Lindo, lindo'.

'That's a bloody stupid name for a kangaroo,' Sally said. She later found out he was talking about her, saying, 'Beautiful, beautiful'.

An hour later it was dark. Neil and I had already demolished six bottles of beer when the truck started up and roared off down the dusty road.

'More beers, bigger men. See you in Huaraz,' Trace and Sally screamed from the cab window, laughing.

To our surprise everyone had sneaked on board the truck and left us behind. The nearest house was thirty kilometres away, Huaraz more than a hundred. In our drunken state we felt sure they would not leave us so we feigned indifference and continued singing.

Sprawled in the middle of a dirt road in Northern Peru, I felt a strong camaraderie with Neil. His wit and energy had become the linchpin holding the expedition together. My feelings were confused by the situation with Trace. But he could hardly be held responsible for the way she felt about him. He did not seem to be either encouraging or discouraging her, just enjoying the attention.

Two more beers and nearly an hour later there was still no sign of the truck. It was getting cold. We only had one layer of clothes on, no money, no water, no food. It was a full night's walk to the nearest house and we were in the middle of a country virtually in a civil war. But still we did not care. To show our defiance we sang more childish songs. Still no truck. The bastards *had* left us.

We stopped singing. I looked around at the black silhouettes of the surrounding mountains. The stars twinkled in the sky, the bracing mountain air helped sober us up. After climbing Pisco we felt sure a thirty kilometre hike would present few problems.

'Better start walking,' I slurred. We set off, beer in hand, weaving down the road like a couple of old drunks on a Friday night.

HUARAZ

17
WELCOME BACK
TO HUARAZ

I don't mind crevasses, avalanches or
frostbite but there is no way I am
going to have you sticking a needle in
my arse.

Neil

W e found the truck hidden behind a bend, two kilometres down the road. I felt a little disappointed. I was
looking forward to the adventure of an all-night hike.

Milton arrived with the donkeys, furious that no one had
stayed behind at Cave Camp to help load. For once none of
us paid him too much attention because, as Trace wrote, we
were all far too drunk.

Neil and Chris did what they always do when they are drunk
together and have an audience. They sing and perform Patricia
the Stripper. *So they danced around in the headlights with gay*
abandon, stripping while they sang. The donkeys were not at all
happy at the bright lights and the terrible sight of frolicking, pale
naked men.

How we ever got everything on to the back of the truck, I will
never know. We were as pissed as farts and as tired as successful
summiteers. Deirdre took the warm front seat. For the rest of us in
the back, the four-hour truck trip to Huaraz was abominable. We
lay in the open air and froze. It made me think what it must have
been like to be a prisoner of war, being taken in an open truck
through a Siberian wasteland.

The most unpleasant journey of our lives was closely

155

followed by the worst meal. We arrived in Huaraz at two in the morning. None of us had eaten properly since breakfast.

The only restaurant open appeared to be hosting a Shining Path convention. Suspicious-looking men crouched around tables, whispering to each other over full ashtrays and empty coffee cups. They didn't seem to consider us a threat, perhaps because we looked as if we too were involved in an armed struggle.

After a few minutes however, some of them shifted to tables further away. I felt a bit embarrassed and assumed we were too rowdy. Later I learned they objected to the stench of sixteen people who had not seen a bar of soap for the last two weeks.

We ordered a variety of inedible food. Most of us left in disgust to go back to the hotel. The waiter showed no surprise that most of the food was untouched and disappeared back into the kitchen with our full bowls, perhaps destined for other tables.

Before I went to bed, I glanced at myself in the mirror. I was horrified by what I saw. My hair was matted, my face badly peeled and pale in some areas, deeply tanned in others. Snot clung to my nose and my lips were very chapped. I was too exhausted to do anything about it that night.

Next morning I woke feeling great. The sensual pleasures on today's agenda were a shower, closely followed by breakfast. Our hotel hot-water system would have fascinated an archaeologist with a specialist interest in ancient plumbing. It probably predated the Incas. In the early hours of the morning it faithfully produced a cacophony of rattling noises but never delivered any hot water.

Instead we filed across the road to the public showers. They were ideologically suspect since the wood-fired boiler was rumoured to be fuelled by trees felled in the Amazon. Judging by the temperature and quantity of the hot water, no sapling in Peru was safe.

I stood in my cubicle, washing and re-washing myself and my clothes, luxuriating in the hot water. I stayed under the shower for a full hour, getting my two-trees' worth. It was here I discovered all the nerve endings at the tips of my toes had been killed by the cold. It must have happened before the first dinner party on Mt Pisco when I tried to get everyone up early. Clearly I had been very close to getting frostbite. Milton had been proved right again.

Our mission in Huaraz was to eat. We desperately needed to replace the fat reserves we had lost on Pisco, before tackling Huascaran. We had three days of hard eating ahead, during which time the mood of the expedition would totally change.

Ordering food at breakfast in the climbers' café was always an ordeal. My Spanish was nonexistent and Neil's no better. He claimed there were only two phrases you needed to survive in any country: 'My friend will pay,' and 'Will this drainpipe hold my weight?'

Sally was the next to burst through the door.

'Great feeding frenzy!' she shouted gleefully, rolling up the sleeves of her three-dollar Peruvian jersey and pushing back her blonde hair in preparation for some serious eating. She ordered chocolate cake, three crêpes, fruit salad and muesli and wolfed the lot inside an hour. It was practically the high point of the expedition for her.

I was in my element. Never before had I been able to eat as much as I liked and not worry about putting on weight. I was guaranteed to lose it on Huascaran.

As the café filled with Social Climbers I became aware of the smell of each individual's perfume, aftershave, washing powder, soap, toothpaste, shampoo and moisturiser. We rolled out of the café an hour later, just in time for lunch.

On the way to a fish restaurant, we were passed repeatedly by Lorenzo and Britannion driving a dilapidated brown VW beetle, with one of the four wheel arches missing.

157

'Hola, hola,' they shouted.

'Hombres Supers,' we shouted back each time.

Milton had paid them that morning and for the next few days they were rich men in a poor town. They celebrated by buying a case of beer and hiring the beetle for a day, and spent the afternoon driving round town, drinking and tooting the horn at their friends.

Milton assured us the fish in the restaurant was fresh so we abandoned all caution. Halfway through lunch I was too stuffed to eat any more so I asked Trace to go for a walk. To my surprise, she agreed. We passed the outskirts of town and walked up a deep valley.

A small stream ran down one side of the narrow valley and those few trees which had escaped the public shower's boiler clung to the valley walls. Trace and I started to talk freely. The only person we never mentioned was Neil, the situation was too volatile.

The valley widened into a small, secluded glade. In the middle of the glade there was an empty stone pool which, judging by the quality of the masonry, looked like Inca handiwork. On a nearby hill, a young boy tended a few goats.

The glade had a strange feeling about it. I imagined pagan rituals might once have taken place there. The scene had affected Trace as well. She sat on the edge of the pool swinging her feet, gazing into the distance in her own dream world.

I stared at her. She had lost so much weight her figure looked more adolescent than ever. The scar on her right thigh had become very pronounced now it was deeply tanned. She looked so vulnerable, which was probably why she was always so assertive, to force people to take her seriously.

She caught me gazing at her and gave me an encouraging smile.

Without thinking, I walked across the pool, bent down,

put my head between her legs and lifted her over my shoulders, upside down, so her face was in the small of my back and her legs stretched in front of me.

I started to spin and hit her on the bottom with a stick. She laughed as we pirouetted around the empty Inca swimming pool, and gently stroked my legs.

I glanced up the hill. The young goat herder watched us intently, not sure what these two gringos were doing. We were both getting very dizzy and turned on. I put her down. Her eyes were wide open and she had a wild smile.

She began to kiss me. I did not know how far she would go. Then I realised this meant nothing to her. It was just another of her games, but I was serious. I pulled away.

'Let's go back,' I muttered.

The spell was broken and the excitement disappeared from her face. I could not work out whether she was disappointed or relieved, she looked like she did not care either way. As we walked back to the hotel in silence, she wandered along behind me, tickling my legs with a long piece of grass.

That night we celebrated Avril's birthday at a restaurant. Glen was the first to be hit by the dreaded rotten egg burps and he knew violent vomiting and diarrhoea would soon follow. Chris rushed him back to the hotel but their departure did not dampen our spirits. Illness was now an accepted fact of life on the expedition. We were not to know the local 'fresh fish restaurant' was about to wreak havoc.

We left the restaurant for a nightclub. Eddie stayed behind, weaving from table to table draining our half-finished beers, wine and Pisco Sours. We never found out what he got up to that night — he certainly couldn't remember.

Trace had been ignoring me all evening. She started dancing with Neil, then switched allegiance to Peru's answer to John Travolta. He had long, jet-black hair and

159

wore a black satin shirt and trendy, torn jeans, set off by a white silk scarf tied around his waist.

I was furious. She was deliberately avoiding me and dancing with someone she had never met before. As is so often the case with jealousy, the wrong person bore the brunt of it. I blamed Juan Travolta.

I was ready to attack him but Wolfgang intervened. The concept of me wrestling on a packed dance floor with the local stud over Trace must have appealed to his Germanic instincts. But only if he had a camera to film it. He did not. So instead he made his most sensible suggestion of the expedition.

'Vy don't you simply dance with her?'

I pushed through the packed dance floor and asked her for a dance. She described what happened.

> *A Peruvian asked me to dance. I spent the next half-hour trying to avoid catching his lecherous eyes. He was a brilliant dancer and I am fascinated by the samba and the way the Peruvian body moves to the rhythm.*
>
> *Halfway through this episode of dirty dancing I was alarmed by a distinct flavour of rotten egg coming from my gut. Oh no, not an eggy burp! Anything but an eggy burp. This was the sign of worse things to come. I escaped from the writhing mass of the Peruvian to the madly waving arms of Chris. Soon I could not ignore the warning bells any longer as my pet amoeba took a grip on my stomach.*
>
> *I rushed back to the hotel and what followed was one of my worst nights ever. The awful dilemma of whether to sit on or lean over the loo. You lose your guts in both directions simultaneously in one rapid expulsion. You are left praying that it will soon be over, though fearing it is only the beginning. God, it was awful.*

At three in the morning Trace came into my room and woke me. She looked pale and weak. She climbed into my bed, while I went to find Glen. I heard him before I saw him. The sounds of people suffering from giardia echoed round the hotel, for once drowning out the rattling of the hot water system.

Glen gave her an injection and a monster pill. She crawled back to her room. An hour later I woke again. This time I could hear Neil being sick in the bathroom. He looked almost as terrible as the bathroom floor, which was covered in vomit.

I found Glen in his bathroom again. In between expulsions he thrust a syringe into my hand and told me to give Neil an injection in the top right hand quadrant of his bum. Having seen the evidence of what Neil's bum was capable of I was not keen to go anywhere near it. Neil was even more horrified by the sight of me standing in the toilet doorway brandishing a syringe.

'I don't mind crevasses, avalanches or frostbite,' he mumbled wiping some vomit off his chin with the back of his hand, 'but there is no way I am going to have you sticking a needle in my arse.'

I went back to bed relieved.

Short of blowing up the hotel, it is doubtful whether the Shining Path could have caused more damage to the expedition than our choice of fish restaurants. Neil, Sally, Trace, Glen, Murf and Eddie had all been hit. Mike was more ill than ever. Jenny had retreated to Buenos Aires with another unknown ailment, later diagnosed as twins.

Eddie's symptoms were similar to Jenny's: morning sickness with bad headaches. Initially, we thought he had contracted a hitherto unknown form of low-altitude sickness but it turned out to be a hangover.

Our departure had to be delayed for a day, to give everyone time to recover. Time was running out.

By the next day Murf had recovered. At breakfast we met an English mountaineering guide who was shocked that a team of total novices were planning to climb Huascaran. She told us that it was nothing like 'a straight walk to the summit'. There were at least three crevasses to cross and five ice walls to climb. Moreover, the weather had been terrible this season and showed no signs of improving.

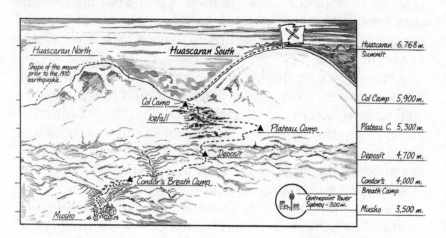

Murf certainly looked the part of an experienced mountaineer wearing his favourite fluffy jacket covered with badges of mountains he had scaled and advanced climbing courses he had passed. I could tell he was very concerned because he stopped stuffing his face. He asked her a range of technical questions, while I sat beside him gravely nodding, pretending to understand what they were discussing. Huascaran was going to be a lot harder than we had expected.

Murf started to formulate plans for Huascaran in the light of this new information. I was relieved he was on the expedition. Milton and Murf worked in very different ways and Neil summed up the difference: 'Milton reacts to situations, while Murf prepares for them.' Fortunately Milton listened to Murf's suggestions.

'I'm pretty pissed off with the expedition organisation,' Murf complained to me. 'There is no way you could describe the food as anything but awful. We should be taking more pasta and more dehydrated food.'

Murf proposed a series of changes for the expedition. We already had one plus in our favour — the De La Crue brothers, who sounded like high-wire artists but were actually two of South America's top mountaineers — had been recruited to our expedition. Nicholas and Sebastian De La Crue promised to be real assets.

Murf wanted us to maximise our advantages by taking more complex carbohydrates, less tuna and vegetable soup, more stoves, less personal gear and fewer dining-room accessories.

The documentary crew had agreed to take less camera equipment. Mike was too ill to come, so Chris and Glen were all that remained of the team. Wolfgang had disappeared to Hawaii, to make a riveting one-hour television special on a little-known but inspired artist who specialised in lowering himself into active volcanoes, under cover of darkness, to create sculptures out of molten lava. I wondered what social comment Wolfgang would find in that?

When I told Milton about the severe conditions on Huascaran he did not look particularly worried or surprised and muttered something about the ice fall opening up since his last climb.

Perhaps he had always known that Huascaran was not a straight walk to the summit. But having guided hundreds of novices up mountains he knew that most people are capable of achieving greater feats of physical endurance than they themselves might imagine. He had built up our confidence on Pisco to prepare us for the much tougher challenge of Huascaran.

Milton called a meeting to brief everybody about the dangers ahead. A summit before the summit was scheduled for the climbers' café that night.

The dark wood panelling of the café enhanced the dramatic atmosphere of the meeting. Milton was decidedly unimpressed by our performance on Pisco. Between mouthfuls of chocolate cake, he listed his grievances. Chief among them was his belief there had been too much 'social' and not enough actual 'climbing'. The guides and porters shouldered most of the loads. People had fallen in crevasses and everyone seemed to have been ill *all* the time. According to Milton we would be damned lucky to get anyone to the summit of Huascaran.

'Look, expect something four to six times harder than Pisco,' Milton said, seriously eyeing each one of us. The humour of the situation was not lost on Sally.

I sat in the café attempting to look confident while trying to conjure up an image four to six times worse. Pisco was minus twenty degrees Celsius, had sixty degree ice climbs, was five thousand eight hundred metres high and we had used only six porters and three stoves.

I'm starting to picture Huascaran. The temperature will be between minus eighty and minus one hundred and twenty degrees Celsius. The whole route up the mountain is a complete overhang. Huascaran must be between twenty-three and thirty-four thousand metres high — not far from the moon — and will only have one-and-a-quarter porters and a fraction of a stove. This is going to be fun.

Milton went round the table and eye-balled each Social Climber individually. 'Can you handle it? Are you still prepared for the consequences?'

No one was prepared to publicly back down now. That would have been too brave an act. It was far easier to mouth confident phrases: 'Sure, no problems', 'Absolutely committed', 'Great, excellent, fantastic'. Secretly we were all thinking: 'How the hell do I know?'

The attack then came from the medical side. Glen gave us a mournful rundown on the physical challenges ahead. He did his best to frighten us.

'Mike was seriously ill on Pisco,' he said lugubriously, 'I mean seriously ill. Pisco was a comparatively easy mountain to evacuate. If Mike had fallen ill on Huascaran, we would have been in deep shit and I mean deep shit.'

We sat impassively and listened. I could see what they were trying to do. They wanted to weed out the weak, to trim the party to a core team of strong, committed members. I particularly watched for Deirdre's reaction but she didn't flinch or show any sign of wanting to drop out. She sat with a stony expression looking deadly determined. I wondered if she was going to prove us all wrong and do it. Often the consequences of failure prove a stronger motivating force than the rewards of success.

Neil announced that from now on everyone would carry their own dining gear and personal effects. No more offloading kit on to other people. It was a pointed reference. Deirdre and I were the only ones guilty of doing this.

We were told every gram could make the difference between success and failure. Watches should be left behind, labels taken off clothes and toothbrushes cut in half. Murf generously offered to make sure I packed the correct half of my toothbrush.

I ducked out for some fresh air. Apparently everyone was still keen and no one was going to be bullied out of this mad adventure. New sleeping arrangements were discussed in my absence. I was in for a shock when I returned to the restaurant.

'Chris, we've worked out the tents for Huascaran,' said Trace, suddenly very friendly. 'I've got some good news.'

I completely misinterpreted this snippet. 'You mean I'm sharing a tent with you?' My eagerness appalled her.

'No, no, you're sharing with Ballantyne and Deirdre. We thought it would make sense to put all the people of the same speed together.' I stared at her in amazement.

It was very hurtful and made no sense at all. Far better to put the strong and the weak ones together so the strong could look after the weak. But that was not the real reason behind the change.

Neil, Avril and Murf were working well together in one

tent. Sally and Eddie were a great team and Trace wanted to go in with them because she gravitated towards strength.

Deirdre's heart did not seem to be in the expedition. We all expected her to pull out at any time. Ballantyne was widely considered to be impossible to sleep with because of his mad-dog antics first thing in the morning. Clearly most people would prefer to share a tent with a rutting llama than spend a night with me.

We were the no-hopers tent. People thought we would never reach the summit and did not want to share with us even if we did. We were no longer Social Climbers, we were social outcasts. Murf privately summarised the prevailing view.

> There is little hope for Chris's tent. Chris has a broken knee, Ballantyne broken ribs and Deirdre a broken will.

I could imagine our nights together at 6000 metres. Three of us crammed into a two-man tent. Deirdre at one end with her cosmetics and private library. Ballantyne quietly juggling ice axes at the other while I thrashed around in the middle in my sleeping bag, kicking the others and muttering in my sleep, 'Trace, Trace, you're the only one for me!'

Suppressing my fury, I quietly slipped away from the climbers' café. I wandered back to the hotel along dimly-lit streets. As I sat miserably in my room I realised the whole mood of the expedition had changed. On Pisco everyone had helped each other but on Huascaran, people were going to be a lot more selfish.

Suddenly the lights went out. Peering through the window I could see the whole town was in darkness. It was the anniversary of the formation of the Shining Path and they loved blowing up power lines on their birthday.

The streets were dark but the mountains surrounding Huaraz looked bright in the full moon. Huascaran domi-

166

nated the other mountains and loomed over the town, seemingly very close, even at a distance of forty kilometres.

Huascaran glowed as if covered in luminous blue paint. It looked serene. I wondered if it would seem so benevolent in a couple of days when we commenced the struggle to the summit.

The expedition had turned deadly serious.

Who would sit at the dinner on the summit of Huascaran?

That was the question the documentary crew wanted to ask me confidentially the following day. I sat on my bed, watching Glen and Chris set up their tripod, trying to decide how to answer it. There seemed to be two separate factors affecting people's chances, physical strength and motivation.

Physically, Trace was on top. She hardly seemed to notice the altitude. Avril and Neil ran a close second, they hardly seemed to notice the discomfort. Deirdre had shown late form when climbing Pisco the second time. Eddie and Sally were both reasonably strong. Murf had been ill a surprising amount of the time but I felt sure his experience would pull him through. Physically, Ballantyne and I were the weakest.

When it came to motivation, the order changed. We all had a lot to lose if we failed to climb the mountain because we had assured our friends, family, media and the experts that we would have the world's highest dinner. If we didn't make it, everyone would lose a lot of face.

Ballantyne and I were by far the most determined to have the dinner party. I knew Neil's pride would drive him to be there and Trace was strongly motivated. Everyone except Trace had a job and a home to go back to whether the expedition succeeded or not. In her life of wandering Trace had few possessions except her clothes, mountaineering gear and youth hostel card. The expedition had become her life and she had thrown all her energies into it from the start. Nothing was going to stop her reaching the summit.

I had less confidence in the others. Would Avril lose interest in her masochistic experiment? Did Murf enjoy training the team and travelling in South America more than actual mountaineering? Would Eddie's interest in the expedition continue to fluctuate? Perhaps Sally might decide it was too dangerous. And how committed was Deirdre?

Based on Milton's claim that climbing mountains is eighty per cent mental and twenty per cent physical, I compiled my short list. I decided Neil, Trace, Avril, Murf, Ballantyne and myself would make it. Sally, I suspected, would decide it was too dangerous and turn back and Eddie would use her as an excuse to give up as well. I felt sure Deirdre could make it if she wanted to but I was not sure she did.

Ironically, this was the same list I made in Australia and I had still only guessed one out of the three correctly. But irrespective of what I thought, the group had made up its own mind and behaviour polarised accordingly.

The less confident ones — Ballantyne, Sally, Deirdre and I — concentrated on preparing for the ordeal ahead. Eddie and Avril were quietly confident. Murf, Trace and Neil were all over confident and behaved like prima donnas. Neil made a book of his summit favourites.

> I think Eddie, Murf, Sally, Avril, Trace and myself will be at the dinner party. Chris had severe physical problems on Pisco and he will find it tough. I've seen Ballantyne turn from a sprightly character into an old man but he is very determined. Deirdre will struggle.

The weight of opinion was against Ballantyne, Deirdre and myself. We met in Ballantyne's room. Deirdre and Ballantyne were both insulted by everyone's lack of confidence in them. It was the first time I'd seen Ballantyne angry.

'We'll make it if we work together as a team,' he fumed, cutting a piece of soap in half to save weight. He looked up and flashed a warm smile to indicate he was not annoyed with us, just with those who thought we would not make it. Deirdre wore a solemn expression which I misinterpreted as determination. Judging by her diary entry she actually felt cornered. On the one hand she felt she should climb Huascaran for Ansett and on the other she dreaded the thought of it.

> *Living on Pisco had been uncomfortable and far from fun. The altitude made me feel lousy — lack of showers, toilets, food, sleep, privacy and general hygiene, not to mention the cold I felt whilst living on the snow.*
>
> *I don't really want to think about Huascaran, what a horrible idea. It is obvious everyone is out for themselves. I thought there would be more team spirit.*

We discussed our plans for the mountain. Between the three of us we would take one first-aid kit, one watch, one tube of toothpaste and a torch, in a desperate bid to lighten our load. As a joke we christened ourselves the 'A Team'. I went back to my room to cut the labels off my clothes. Neil and Murf kept interrupting me.

'Now Chris,' Murf joked, 'Neil and I want to know if the A Team stands for the Arseholes Team?' I politely laughed.

Neil picked up my camera from my bed. I took it back from him.

'Ugly, why don't you leave your lens caps this time to save weight?'

They walked out laughing. I was usually prepared to laugh at this type of ribbing but by now my confidence was low. Murf returned and trod on a very raw nerve.

'Chris, by the way,' he said with a smile, 'we've formed "The Mission Impossible Team" to get you laid, now that Trace has dumped you.'

I completely lost control of myself.

169

'Fuck off!' I yelled, jumping across the room to attack him. Like all good soldiers, Murf knew when to retreat. He sprinted down the corridor and locked himself in his room.

I felt incredibly embarrassed. In Australia I had insisted no shouting would be allowed, now I was the first to break my own rule. There was a knock on the door and Trace came in, unaware of what had just happened.

'There is a member of the Shining Path waiting for you at reception,' she joked.

I stared at her condescendingly.

'Go away Trace,' I sneered. She left looking confused and hurt.

I felt even worse — she had not deserved that. When I went down the corridor to apologise, I found her neatly folding her clothes on her bed. She looked sad. She realised Murf and Neil had been teasing me because she had rejected me. I returned to my room and decided to put all the politics of the expedition to the back of my mind. There were more important things to consider.

We were advised because of terrorist activity to delay our departure until four the next morning. So we had lost another half day. In recent months the situation had got out of hand in Huaraz. Our beer truck driver had survived a bomb being thrown into his house the day before his wedding and two restaurants had been blown up. Having your restaurant destroyed was actually a compliment, the equivalent of a five-star rating in a dining out guide. The Shining Path only blew up the best restaurants in town, they probably owned the cheaper ones.

The tension was escalating. An English tourist had been shot dead, power lines were being sabotaged and Huaraz was now swarming with soldiers. An armed guard, with a machine gun, was stationed outside our hotel.

I never thought I would consider the mountains as a place of safety but I could not wait to get out of Huaraz. Everyone except Avril felt the same way. She was too pragmatic to be intimidated by such a shadowy menace and when she did acknowledge the existence of these ruthless revolutionaries, she referred to them as 'busy little bees'.

Her attitude proved to be the correct one. We never saw any terrorists, so Neil dubbed them 'guerrillas in the mist'.

Mt Huascaran

18
OUR EVEREST

The mountain was enormous and that shook me up. Who am I doing it for?

Deirdre

Milton had originally allowed twenty-three days to climb Huascaran, to give us enough time for two separate summit attempts. Now there were only nine days left, barely enough time for one attempt, weather permitting.

At four in the morning we began loading the truck. It was still dark, the temperature just above freezing. Deirdre commandeered the warm cab seat. The rest of us jumped into the open back of the truck with all the food, leaking fuel cans, now-battered dining furniture, and mountaineering gear.

We had learned a lesson from the last freezing truck trip. We huddled in a communal bed, collectively covered by unzipped sleeping bags laid together to form an enormous doona. It must have looked like a medieval painting of a poor family, sixteen children tucked up in one bed. Soon we were all asleep as the truck bounced up the dirt road towards the mountain village of Musho, two hours away.

An hour out of Huaraz, I woke up. I wriggled out from the warmth and balanced on the wooden side of the truck. We zig-zagged into the foothills, meandering towards the strengthening orange glow of the approaching dawn. Every

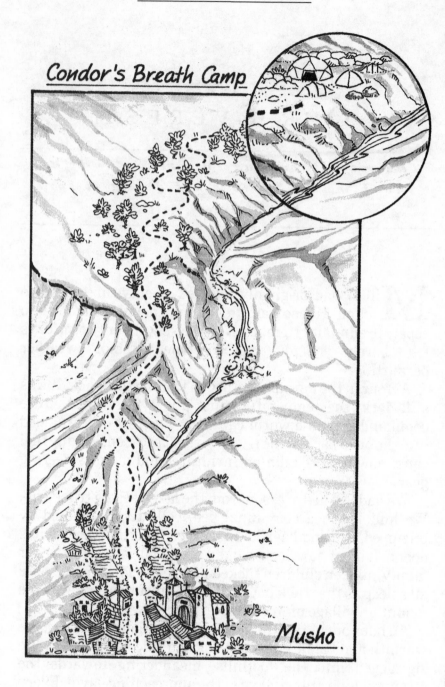

Condor's Breath Camp

Musho

now and again I had a brief glimpse of Huascaran.

The sight of the mountain gave me butterflies. Niggling worries formed inside my head. What had I forgotten? What would go wrong? If the loads became too heavy, which dinner-party items would we dump? If we failed on this bid who would stay to give it another try? How could I afford a second attempt anyway?

Pisco had just been the training mountain. Huascaran was much higher and we now knew it was going to be much more difficult. To a Tim Macartney-Snape or a Chris Bonington, Huascaran would have been a relatively simple climb. But to us, Huascaran was Everest.

We drove into Musho in the soft pre-dawn light. Musho was badly named but otherwise the kind of picturesque, remote Peruvian village promised in tourist brochures. Small plaster-and-wood houses with brown tiled roofs, no cars but plenty of donkeys parked outside. A couple of pigs scampered out of our way as the truck roared through the village kicking up a cloud of dust. In true Spanish style, the village square was dominated by an oversized white church dwarfing the meagre houses.

At the top of the village we stopped outside a small cream house. A rusty Coca-Cola sign nailed to the cracked front wall was the only indication that it was the village café. Musho was completely deserted at this early hour.

Huascaran for once was not shrouded in cloud. It stood so much higher than the surrounding peaks it looked aloof. Shaped like an enormous capital 'M' or as Murf pointed out, two breasts, it dominated the village. I could see where half the mountain had 'fallen off' in the 1970 earthquake, burying the 30 000 inhabitants of Huaraz, as if someone had taken a large bite out of the left hand side of the 'M'.

The intense level of involvement necessary to climb a mountain leads to strange ideas among committed mountaineers. They often become convinced that each peak has its own personality. It is not, they will tell you, a question of whether you will climb the mountain, it is whether the mountain will allow you to climb it. Looking up at Huascaran I could see what they were on about. The mountain seemed to be glaring back at me. Yet rationally I knew this was nonsense, mountains are just enormous piles of frozen rock.

Others too were aware of Huascaran's aura. Deirdre expressed her first reactions.

> *The mountain was enormous and that shook me up. Who am I doing it for? It is not an ego trip for me and it certainly isn't fun either. I felt a responsibility to Ansett which in Huaraz outweighed all the other ifs and buts. But looking at the mountain I felt differently. It was going to be a lot more testing, more uncomfortable and a lot less fun. I cannot understand what each person's motivation is in doing it. Maybe it is to prove how tough they are.*

Sally's confidence was also rocked by the sight of the mountain.

> *I wonder what it would be like to just stop but I cannot imagine myself doing it. We have been told that above 6200 metres things get a lot worse, not 100 metres by 100 metres but metre by metre. The body wastes away, it is much colder and the level of oxygen decreases rapidly. I've done one mountain and I'll give this everything so if I don't make it at least I'll know I've done my best.*

We unloaded the truck and it turned around and slowly drove off. I half expected someone to break from the group and sprint after it, shouting, 'Don't leave me, don't leave me!' No one did. We all watched the only form of escape gather speed and disappear down the dusty road.

One type of transport was replaced by another. A caravan of thirty donkeys was herded down the road by local children for Lorenzo and the donkey handlers to load. The process took ages because Lorenzo was still drunk from the night before and kept sneaking behind the café to top up his already stratospheric blood-alcohol level with beer.

The local kids soon tired of watching him stagger and turned their attention to us. I had not expected Peruvian children to look so well. Before the expedition I mentally prepared myself for the sight of starving children on street corners. We never saw the slums in Lima but in the countryside almost everybody looked healthy.

The village barber obviously only had two pudding bowls: one for the boys and a second, with a section cut out at the back, for the girls' long hair. Track suits were the fashion, with traditional coloured shawls and grubby brown jerseys as optional extras. They could have been kids from almost any western country waiting for something to happen.

Chris Hilton fired up the documentary camera and the Social Climbers' circus performed for them. They watched, mesmerised, as Ballantyne began spinning plates on sticks and juggling coloured balls, delighted by the antics of a clown old enough to be their grandfather. None of them spoke English but Ballantyne maintained his normal stream of patter.

'Ladies and Gentlemen, you will notice that at no time do my fingers leave my hands,' he announced. This spiel was delivered with a fixed showman's grin. 'Don't clap, just throw money,' he said as they applauded each act.

Eddie and Neil were the support acts. Eddie gave each excited kid a pink or yellow nose with Le Zinc sunblock. Neil gave them piggyback rides.

'Huascaran looks like a friendly mountain, doesn't it?' Neil gasped, before sprinting off down the dirt road with another screaming kid bouncing around on his back.

To Deirdre, there was nothing 'friendly-looking' about the mountain. I became aware that she was standing beside me while I photographed Ballantyne. At first glance she looked her neat, cosmetic self. The collar of her red fluffy jacket was up and her hair was carefully plaited. But she had a fiercely-determined expression on her face.

'I've decided I'm not going to climb Huascaran,' she stated. 'I'm not enjoying it and my mother is ill in Australia and I want to go back home.'

I was amazed she had travelled for two hours, at such an early hour, to a remote village with no telephones and no cars and waited till our truck had left, before announcing that her mother was ill and needed her in Australia.

I stared at her for a second. I did not want to dissuade her. She was clearly more determined not to climb Huascaran than some of the others were to climb it.

'Chris, don't make a fuss of this,' she insisted.

She meant she did not want to be interviewed by the documentary crew. I could not face a scene, so meekly I agreed. Jim discreetly arranged for Nicholas De La Crue to walk her back to the main road, fifteen kilometres away, where they could hitchhike back to Huaraz.

It was a strange sight watching her walk down the dirt track, Nicholas carrying her pack. She passed Ballantyne juggling, Neil still giving rides and Eddie playing with the local kids. She was too embarrassed to say goodbye to anyone.

Deirdre was the only one who had not lost sight of the fact that the whole expedition was supposed to be a light-hearted joke. The rest of us had slowly accepted that climbing Huascaran was going to be unbelievably tough and potentially lethal.

She had started from a different standpoint from everyone else. She had applied to join the expedition on the strength of a frivolous ad on a notice board and joined a group which had been training together for many months. Her sense of isolation was made worse by the unexpectedly appalling conditions she faced on the mountain.

Everyone on the expedition had a point beyond which they would not go, a level determined by how well they coped with the traumas of mountaineering and the strength of their personal commitment. All the other Social Climbers had paid at least $3000 to come on the expedition and some had put in a year's work. Deirdre did not have that commitment. Ansett had paid all her costs and she had joined the expedition so late she was never able to contribute to the planning. She had already climbed Pisco twice for Ansett, which was probably twice more than she had wanted. I did not blame her for leaving.

News broke that Deirdre had slipped away. Sally felt guilty and wished we had been more supportive. Trace and Eddie were annoyed about her lack of commitment. Neil was angry because I had not alerted the documentary crew for a final interview. But soon it was agreed that her departure was for the best.

We set off up the mountain with the local kids drifting along behind, hoping for more entertainment. We had a day's leisurely stroll ahead of us. There was not a breath of wind or a cloud in the sky. It felt like a summer's ramble after Sunday lunch.

The path followed the main stream, cascading off Huascaran through terraced fields. The steeper it became, the smaller the fields were until finally they gave way to forest.

Only a few weeks earlier we had all been gasping for air at 3700 metres. Just as our tanned faces could now withstand the harsh sunlight, our bodies had adapted to the rarefied atmosphere. This walk now seemed only a little harder than walking at sea level.

There were still a few ailments in the group. Neil, Trace and Avril had piles. Sally and Murf were suffering from giardia. Murf was riding a horse to save energy and looked a bit out of control as he trotted past.

'I hope I don't lose me guts with all this bouncing around,' he muttered. I was sure the horse agreed with him.

Trace was in one of her poetic mountain moods. It was fairly obvious I was not wanted so I left her with Neil (Photo 39).

Jim made the mistake of leaving Sally, Eddie and Avril to their own devices. Now they were nowhere to be seen. To be lost already was a spectacular achievement, even by our impeccable standards of incompetence. Jim had carefully pointed out where the camp site was and there was only one route to reach it. He offered a large reward of one dollar to the first Peruvian kid to locate them. They scampered back down the track shouting in glee.

'Hola Salle, hola Eddee!'

An hour later, one of them smart enough to commandeer a bicycle, found Sally, Avril and Eddie striding out in totally the wrong direction. Only after frantic gesticulations was he able to prevent them from climbing some other unpronounceable mountain in neighbouring Bolivia. They were herded back to Jim. From then on Jim ceased to treat any of us like intelligent human beings and insisted that we stick together.

Walking that day was a pleasure. I had a full view of Huascaran looming above me. Surely now I would be inspired to pen a paragraph of purple prose about our mountain, in the tradition of the great mountaineering books. Something like:

> She stands like a Goddess, defying those who would set sacrilegious feet on her unsullied shrine.
> W.E. Bowman, The Ascent of Rum Doodle

> Chomolungma lorded over the divine mountains, her dizzy head circled by a halo of clouds.
> Sorrel Wilby, Beyond the Icefall.

I felt inadequate. Whenever I looked at Huascaran only two words came to mind. Big and cold.

There were two unanswered questions. How dangerous was it? And would we lose anyone? Mountaineering books often read like obituary columns. One in ten people who stand on the summit of Everest never return. Moreover, death on mountains is not confined to the world's highest peaks, both Pisco and Huascaran have claimed lives recently.

I am embarrassed to admit that I actually considered whether a death on the expedition might help the project's media potential. In the end I realised no one would believe it was worth dying for a dinner on top of a mountain. Unless that person was me. In which case they would consider it poetic justice, the obsessed leader perishing for his bizarre expedition: an epitaph to surrealism.

Neil was also becoming dangerously obsessed. 'If I die after I get to the top,' he told the documentary crew, 'please don't feel sorry for me because I'll be happy when I do.'

It was late afternoon. The rust-coloured bark of the trees beside the steep zigzag track glowed red as sunset approached. Just below camp, Chris Hilton was interviewing Ballantyne for the documentary.

Now that Wolfgang had left, the tone of the documentary had changed. Chris and Glen hated the etiquette theme almost as much as we did. They believed the expedition was bizarre enough without adding inappropriate social comment.

Chris understood obsessions perfectly well. He had spent a year meticulously planning an attempt to become the first person to climb Sydney's 300 metre Centrepoint Tower. He started his ascent before dawn but was spotted by police as he neared the top and fully expected to be pounced on by squads of burly policemen. When he reached his goal he found it deserted.

As the police came up in the lifts, he sprinted down the fire stairs. He burst out into Market Street, to find five police cars with blue lights flashing but not a policeman in sight. There was no point hanging around, so he caught the bus home.

I reached camp just before sunset. Glen and Milton had not come to the mountain with us. Earlier that day they had bribed the hospital in Huaraz to perform an emergency blood test on Mike. It turned out that he probably had made mountaineering history by climbing a 5700 metre mountain with malaria. We had come very close to losing him.

Milton and Glen were just about to set off for the mountain when Deirdre and Nicholas walked into the hotel. Glen persuaded her not to return to Australia but to stay and nurse Mike. She also agreed to a final documentary interview to explain why she had decided not to climb Huascaran.

It was so big, as big as Chris Darwin's ego.

19
CONDOR'S BREATH

*If I had a horse with legs like those
I'd shoot it.*

Avril

'The "Hawaii Five O" team is Murf, Avril and me,'
Neil enthusiastically told the camera. 'We are
racy, successful and like beaches. What the hell we are
doing on a mountain I don't know.'

He bounced around in front of the camera, surrounded by
a chaotic sea of vital equipment. His sleeping bag, jackets
and thermals were strewn over an area normally occupied
by three tents.

Wearing a fixed documentary smile, Union Jack shorts
and a top hat, he boldly expounded various theories about
the expedition. Fearing they might run out of film the
camera team moved on to interview the 'Summit Busters',
Eddie, Trace and Sally. Group morale was at its highest
ever and everyone was bubbling with confidence.

For the first time on the expedition I felt we were all
performing like mountaineers. The tension in Huaraz had
evaporated as we got stuck into achieving our goal. The day
before we had been rejoined by Glen, Milton and Nicholas
and had spent the whole day portering equipment from this
camp, known as Condor's Breath Camp, to Deposit Camp.
Condor's Breath was so named because of the exaggerated
stories about how close these giant birds were swooping

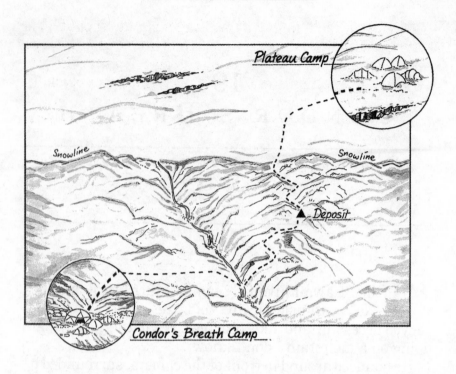

above us on the mountain, close enough, we joked, to feel their hot breath.

Today we were moving up above the snowline to Plateau Camp. It was another beautiful day. I decided to wear my Mickey Mouse shorts, revealing pale, emaciated knobbly knees. Neil spotted Ballantyne and me leaving camp.

'Ahhhh, the intrepid A Team are going for the summit push,' he shouted.

We pretended not to hear him but unfortunately we took the wrong turn and were forced to retrace our steps.

'Hold on!' he continued, 'they're lost already, after only twenty steps.'

'No, they've just stopped for a cigarette break,' Eddie joined in.

Avril could not take her eyes off my spindly legs. 'If I had a horse with legs like those, I'd shoot it.'

Everyone, including Ballantyne and me, burst out laughing. Avril was the master of the one-liner. I had always found her enigmatic to say the least. In the group she was constantly laughing and making dry jokes about chickens and Peruvian terrorists but I found her very hard to talk to one to one. Every time I spoke to her it felt like we'd only just met.

Sally and Avril appeared to be very close but as Sally wrote in her diary her efforts to get to know Avril were blocked.

> *Avril is a very private person. I always knew that but it still*
> *disappoints me. When you get to know someone you expect to hear*
> *their personal thoughts but Avril rarely opens up.*

Neil had been sharing with Avril right from the start of the expedition and had a simpler theory: 'Avril seems to like horses more than humans'. The documentary crew also got nowhere in their efforts to fathom her. When they asked the rest of us what the worst part of the expedition was, we'd all moan about the cold, the food and the danger. Avril had other fears.

> *The worst part of the expedition is when someone farts in the tent*
> *or when Murf threatens to spill his pee bottle on me.*

The path from Condor's Breath to Deposit Camp ran up a series of steep rock steps made smooth by glaciation during the last ice age. Half an hour out of camp, Ballantyne, the documentary crew and I reached a particularly tricky section, where the path traversed a steep slope falling away to our right, made harder to negotiate by the icy conditions.

Ballantyne walked in front of me. Suddenly, he slipped on a sheet of ice and fell, his left shoulder smashing into the ground with a sickening crunch. He had fallen into the steepest, most slippery section and could not stop himself from sliding sideways down into a smooth gully, shaped like a water slide. As a trained acrobat he reacted instinctively. Tumbling down the gully, he managed to push off with one foot and turn his body around. He slid on his pack, feet first, gathered speed and shot out of sight. We heard a splash as he came to rest in an icy pool, some ten metres below.

For a fraction of a second the mountain seemed still. Then the screaming started. He screamed and screamed and screamed. I can still recall the exact pitch of that chilling expression of fear and pain. It stunned me.

Chris Hilton and Glen were more experienced in dealing with emergencies. They had already thrown their packs off and were leaping down the slope towards the noise. As I followed, I was relieved their reaction was to help rather than film. There are cameramen who would choose to keep the film rolling.

Ballantyne lay curled up in the icy pool, soaked to the bone, his silver hair matted to his forehead, eyes tightly shut and his mouth snarled as he fought the pain. He was panting as hard as if he had just run a hundred metre sprint. It was a fear reaction.

'Can you move your arm?' Glen asked urgently. He tried.

'Shit!', he screamed in renewed pain. Evidently not.

Gently we lifted him out of the pool and laid him on the smooth rock. He was shivering with cold as Glen carefully inspected his shoulder.

'It's gone numb,' Ballantyne mumbled, clearly in shock.

Glen diagnosed a ripped rotator cuff in his shoulder. I realised this was the end of the expedition for Ballantyne. First he had cracked two ribs, then his ulcer had started playing up, now effectively he had lost the use of one arm. Glen administered some painkillers. Ballantyne detected we had given up on him and was in no mood for sympathy.

'You don't think I'll make it,' he accused. We all looked a bit embarrassed. 'Even if I have to crawl up, I'll still get to the top of the mountain.'

I was stunned by his determination. Most people his age want to take life easy. He was behaving as if it was a matter of life and death to reach the summit. We had all totally lost sight of the fact that the whole idea was supposed to be a joke.

Despite severe pain he refused to go down. There was no point arguing with him. Lorenzo happened to be passing, carrying another enormous load, and thought nothing of hoisting Ballantyne's pack over one shoulder and continuing up the mountain. As I watched Lorenzo's skinny frame struggling over the rock terraces, I realised how weak we were by comparison.

Glen made a sling out of Ballantyne's scarf and we plodded slowly on up to join the others at the Deposit Camp, where our equipment was stockpiled. The plan was to have lunch, walk up to the snowline a kilometre away, then tackle the final two kilometre snow slog to Plateau Camp.

We sat on the rocks in a feeding frenzy, knowing both our digestive powers and the standard of food would deteriorate dramatically from here on. Tins of peaches, Nestlés milk, jam, biscuits, pasta, tuna fish and water were all consumed in any combination. Murf took me aside for a private chat.

'There is no way Ballantyne is going to make it,' he stated, slurping another tin of peaches.

I agreed, although I hated giving up on him. We had made a pact in Huaraz to help each other to the summit. It unnerved me to think that the expert predictions were coming true. No one thought Deirdre, Ballantyne and I would make it and after only three days it was already two down. I stared at Murf's jam-and-peach encrusted moustache, bouncing up and down as he outlined his plan and ate at the same time. His manner had changed after Pisco. Whereas before everything had been a joke and a laugh, now he was deadly serious. I realised he knew that we were in for a tough time.

'I think the chances are at least one other won't make it,'

189

he predicted, not looking up. I knew who he was thinking of. 'So I'll be the butler for dinner and we'll cut the table and accessories down to six people.'

Our table had been designed in sections so it could be reduced if there were expedition casualties. Already we had dumped a lot of the dining accessories from the Pisco dinner and now only had one glass each, no candelabras, no drinks tray, one bottle of Hardy's wine, no silver service platter and dome and no napkins.

Covertly, we tried to remove extra table sections, plates and cutlery from their boxes. Ballantyne spotted us and knew what was going on.

'Just checking nothing has been broken,' I lied, feeling even more guilty.

Everyone started moving off towards the snowline. Milton banned Ballantyne from going any higher unless his shoulder improved overnight. Ballantyne quietly pleaded with Glen to give a good medical report to Milton but the good doctor was evasive. For his own safety, Glen did not want him on a dangerous glacier with only one arm working. I stayed chatting to Ballantyne trying to cheer him up.

'We've got to get you up to Plateau Camp tomorrow,' I told him. As long as his steely determination remained I would support him.

We experimented to see how much movement he could get into his left arm. Glen had totally strapped the heavily bruised shoulder to prevent upper-arm movement while still allowing some weak movement in the forearm. Ballantyne assured me, with a fake smile and a series of optimistic platitudes, this his arm would recover overnight.

The last of the expedition, Neil, Trace, Sally and Eddie set off. All except Neil ignored us. We had slipped to the status of second-class citizens; now I knew what Deirdre's isolation must have felt like. My suggestion that they should wear Reeboks until the snowline was also ignored, as they set off in heavy, inflexible mountaineering boots.

I kept a close eye on their progress while chatting to Ballantyne. After half a kilometre they were paying the price for wearing mountaineering boots and choosing a different route from the one recommended by Milton. I watched for twenty minutes as they made several unsuccessful attempts to climb a small cliff, realising if I took Milton's route and wore my Reeboks I might beat them to the snowline.

I threw on my pack and set off. My knee had finally strengthened and for the first time I started to climb at a reasonable pace. They were still well ahead but I could see Neil constantly waiting. Someone was exhausted.

I caught them at the snowline. Trace was the cause of their slow progress. She sat slumped on a rock, staring at the ground. Her face was hidden under dark glasses, a woollen hat and white scarves, but her limp body and uncharacteristically quiet manner showed her level of exhaustion. The Goddess at Altitude was losing her shine.

Neil had already taken some of her gear and I took some more. I had raced to catch them up and needed a rest. They left me, Neil and Eddie their normal boisterous selves, Sally quiet and Trace labouring behind, trudging into the soft orange post-sunset glow.

There were still another two kilometres before Plateau Camp. At my speed it would take at least two hours. Trace was usually one of the fastest in the group but up ahead I could see she was suffering. She wrote about the experience in her diary.

The slog to Plateau Camp was terrible. My legs felt like concrete piles. My pack seemed absurdly heavy, it was a grunt all the way. I wasn't meant to be feeling rotten, so what has gone wrong? When I eventually arrived at the camp I was totally pooped and headed for an empty tent. It was minus ten degrees Celsius and all I could think about was getting into my sleeping bag and trying to get warm ... I've sent out a call for Chris as I think he can probably be persuaded to give me a hot cuddle.

I was in no position to give anyone a hot cuddle. It was dark, I had been walking up through the snow for two hours, resting after every thirty paces, with still no sign of camp. My rests became progressively longer. Finally I stopped altogether and sat crumpled in the snow.

I was surrounded by a sea of grey velvet waves of snow, illuminated only by the moon. The double peaks of Huascaran loomed over my shoulder.

I could sense I was being stalked by exhaustion. I had read about it in mountaineering books but only vaguely recognised the symptoms in my dazed state. When you get very tired at altitude not only does the body pack up but the brain stops functioning properly as well. I tried to talk to myself but constant hyperventilating had so affected my vocal cords, my voice was nothing more than a pathetic whisper. I lost the will to go on because I could not see camp and so had no target to aim for.

I felt lethargic and indifferent about my situation. Two opposing voices droned inside my head.

'Stay where you are,' exhaustion whispered to me. 'It is a beautiful starry night.'

'Stand up immediately and get on with it,' commonsense ordered weakly.

'Don't panic,' exhaustion muttered. 'Tenzing will come down soon ... and take your pack ... just wait another ten minutes.'

I waited. The colder I became the more persuasive the voice of exhaustion seemed. A new thought drifted into my consciousness. One from far-left field.

'Maybe Trace put the last bottle of wine in my pack ... maybe it will freeze! Maybe the bottle will crack ... We will have no wine at the dinner then! That cannot happen ...

I've got to get to camp as soon as possible and get it warm.'

I struggled, like a drunkard, to get my pack on and using my ski stocks to stop myself from falling, shuffled off up towards the camp. Walking immediately warmed my body and I started to think straight again. I remembered Milton had the bottle of Hardy's wine and knew he must not find out how close I had come to giving up. If he had been forced to send out a search party for me, I might have been banned from going any higher.

An hour later I staggered into camp. Sally was walking to her tent and when I tried to call her, a rush of air came out but no sound. My vocal cords had given up again. She noticed me.

'Trace has saved a space in her tent for you,' she called, disappearing into her own tent.

I stood in the snow trying to decide what to do. Trace was the last person I wanted to share with. I wandered down to report in to Milton. The light from his hurricane lamp made his tent glow orange as he waited up for me.

'How're you doing, mate?' he jovially welcomed me.

I scoffed down some onion soup and tepid water. He watched me intently as I ate, trying to judge my level of exhaustion to determine how much higher I could go.

'I want to show you something,' he said gently.

We walked to the far side of the camp where he pointed out a narrow crevasse, no wider than the width of my boot, running the whole length of one side of the camp. It brought home the fact that there was now no safe place on the mountain. Under the deceptive snow cover there could be hidden crevasses anywhere, something which would soon be dramatically demonstrated.

Milton retreated to his tent leaving me to ponder where to sleep. Our dark tents were silhouetted against pale snow. Nothing moved apart from a few clouds lazily drifting in from the Amazon.

I had no choice. If I moved in with someone else it would

insult Trace, which she did not deserve.

'How are you doing, Chris?' she enthusiastically greeted me, as I entered the darkness inside the tent.

'Terrible,' I muttered, crawling into my sleeping bag. There was a long silence.

'Do you want to chat?' she asked.

I didn't answer. She had been cheated of her hot cuddle, I was drifting into sleep.

20
THE LEMMING SCHOOL
OF MOUNTAINEERING

I've got this bottle of champagne
thawing between my legs, for later.

Trace

An uninformed condor soaring above Plateau Camp would have been confused by the morning's activities. Five men, wrapped in ropes, were confidently, albeit slowly, trudging up towards the equivalent of a mountain minefield — the icefall.

Three other men, singing 'New York, New York', were walking down the mountain from Plateau Camp. A grandfather, with one arm in a sling, was defiantly shuffling up towards Plateau Camp from Deposit Camp.

At camp, a documentary camera crew and stills photographer avidly filmed a semi-naked emaciated woman, sitting on a fake Louis XIV chair with a champagne bottle tucked, phallus-like, between her legs (Photo 41).

Trace adjusted the bottle of Louis Roederer snugly against her thighs, leaned back in her chair and grinned lewdly at the cameras. She was sunbathing at 5300 metres. She had removed her top and covered her severely depleted breasts with a makeshift 'boob tube'. She claimed her breasts had eloped to Bali along with our libidos.

'I've got this bottle of champagne thawing between my legs, for later,' she announced, making no attempt to conceal the double meaning. Trace enjoyed shocking people

195

with her imaginary perversions.

Plateau Camp was situated on a flat area of the glacier, surrounded by a maze of crevasses. There were only two safe exits and Milton made it very clear that no one should wander anywhere else.

I set off after Neil, Murf and Eddie, to porter food up from Deposit Camp. Sally stopped me.

'Would it be all right if Avril, Trace and I have a day off portering to regain our strength?' she meekly asked.

She did not look very ill. Her blonde hair was neatly plaited and the colour had returned to her face after a bout of giardia. But she knew I would acquiesce for three reasons.

Firstly, I had an appalling record of portering. It would have been hypocritical of me to insist they go down. Secondly, I always found her gentle manner very persuasive. And she knew it. Finally, she was pandering to my cracked ego by asking my permission rather than speaking to Murf or Neil, who had taken over the leadership from me in everything but name. I gave in immediately.

I set off down the mountain to collect more supplies from Deposit Camp. For once I enjoyed the feeling of an empty pack. At sea level, walking downhill is twice as easy as going up; at altitude it is ten times easier.

I met Ballantyne struggling up the mountain. He had not asked Milton's permission to move up to Plateau Camp, knowing it might be refused. His arm was in a sling and he was obviously in pain, his shoulder so damaged he needed help even to take his pack off. We sat in the snow drinking water. He claimed that with heavy strapping he could use his forearm a little. After a few minutes I hoisted his fifteen kilo pack on his back and watched him continue his slow slog up the mountain. An extraordinary man.

An hour later I reached Deposit Camp. Neil, Eddie and Murf were sitting on rocks gulping tins of condensed milk and peaches. Murf's condition had deteriorated over the last day. Hyperventilating had opened his throat to infection again and he now had a constant, dry, hacking cough. This made the controlled breathing required for climbing very difficult. He had completely lost his normal jovial manner.

'Are the girls far behind you?' Murf asked, not looking up from the essential business of eating.

I mumbled evasively, then admitted they were having a rest day. They all stopped eating and stared at me in disbelief. I did not have the guts to tell them I had okayed it.

'What!' Murf shouted before breaking into a coughing fit. 'Right, I'll give those lazy tarts a piece of my mind during the twelve o'clock radio call.' He reacted strongly because he was ill himself but was making the effort.

Neil offered to back him up. He looked at me and remembered the theoretical chain of command. 'Ugly, is it all right if we make the call?'

'Er, yes, er you do it,' I muttered, pretending to concentrate on something far more important. I was relieved not to have to make the call.

At Plateau Camp the women were equally embarrassed. Chris Hilton was grilling them for the camera as they sat in a semi-circle.

'The guys have gone down to get more food and you're being waited on,' he prodded them.

There was a stunned silence. 'You arsehole,' Avril muttered and laughed.

'Am I helping your guilt?' Chris prompted. Like all good interviewers he was trying to provoke a response.

'We might be more useful to the team if we are stronger,' Sally half-heartedly suggested.

'Do you think it would be useful if the guys feel stronger?' No one answered. The stage was now set for a confrontation during the midday radio call.

Up above Plateau Camp, Milton and his guides were setting up fixed ropes through the icefall. An icefall is

197

basically a waterfall of ice, produced when a glacier tumbles over a cliff, consisting of a series of crevasses and ice walls which are forever opening, closing, avalanching and breaking.

The Everest icefall is probably the most dangerous part of that famous mountain. Every year it claims lives. Huascaran's is not nearly as severe but had still managed to claim five lives in an avalanche in the past year. For the expedition to cross quickly and safely, Milton needed to set up ropes over each crevasse and ice wall. It was an exhausting task.

Down at the Deposit Camp we waited for Milton's call.

'It's a bit dangerous,' his voice boomed out of the radio. I could imagine him shouting into the set while hanging on to a rope in a crevasse.

'It's a windslab.' (I never discovered what a windslab was despite having several pointed out to me.) 'Jim's going through the windslab into the soft shit underneath ... It's bloody hard work but ... it's unlikely to avalanche.'

I was beginning to learn to read between the lines with Milton. His talent in the art of understatement was almost as advanced as his talent for safe mountaineering. His choice of words worried me: 'a bit dangerous', 'bloody hard work' and 'unlikely to avalanche'. But I had learned to keep my mouth shut. Anyway, this was the only route up the mountain.

Murf grabbed the radio. 'Plateau Camp, Plateau Camp, this is Deposit.'

'Hello Deposit,' Trace answered in a silly voice, evidently amused that Murf had called himself a deposit. Her flippancy did not help the situation.

Murf's normally lighthearted manner was replaced by rage. 'Youse bloody girls!' he shouted. 'Get your lazy arses into gear, get down here immediately or there is a chance that the expedition will fail. We need food up. We cannot carry it all ourselves!'

There was a long pause. Then Trace did the mountain equivalent of slamming down the telephone — she switched the radio off. Murf stared furiously at the silent handset, muttered something unrepeatable and started coughing again.

Trace radioed back to say they were on their way down. Neil took control and, with characteristic diplomacy, he smoothly defused the situation.

'Yes, of course we understand you're exhausted,' he soothed. 'But remember, no one said it was going to be easy. The success of the expedition relies on everyone's work.'

I listened to this exchange, totally embarrassed. I filled up my pack with food and started walking towards the snowline. Soon my guilt was thankfully replaced by the narcotic effect of extreme exertion.

By late afternoon everyone was back up at Plateau Camp. The sun set sulkily behind the swirling clouds sweeping in from the Amazon. We stood in a huddle, like a flock of emperor penguins in an Antarctic winter. Another inevitable meeting.

Everyone wore their duvet jackets with hoods up against the icy-cold wind, a product of the deteriorating weather. It was strange to think that only seven hours earlier Trace had been sunbathing.

Milton asked whether we thought the expedition should attempt to climb the icefall tomorrow. A question which left me dumbfounded. Murf was ill in his tent and the rest of us knew as much about climbing icefalls as we did about leaping naked into active volcanos.

Puffing out our chests we asked intelligent questions. What was going to happen to the weather? How much fuel did we have? If we had a rest day would it matter? Neil and I were particularly fond of making technical-sounding inquiries. We had read all the mountaineering books and here was an opportunity to make our first mountaineering decision. I was grateful that Milton answered all our questions promptly. He said he didn't know.

By the end we had confused everyone, including Milton. Subconsciously we decided the best way to spread the blame on a bad decision was to put it to the vote.

It was a textbook example of the lemming effect. Everyone voted for the solution demonstrating the most bravado, rather than taking the commonsense option. The decision was to attack the icefall tomorrow. We scurried blindly off towards our metaphorical precipice.

I sat in my tent preparing to depart at two-thirty the following morning. As I tried to organise my camera gear in the failing light I had a sinking feeling we had made a terrible mistake. Although we were very short of time it seemed ridiculous to set off into a blizzard. Half an hour later Milton rectified our error. The departure was cancelled and the next day would be a rest day. It was the first time Milton had given us the power of decision, and thankfully the last.

'Good morning ladies and gentlemen,' Neil announced to the film camera. 'We are gathered here today for one of the premier sporting occasions of the eighties, the official attempt on the Champagne Cork Flight Distance Record.'

We were staging a joke effort to crack another world record for the benefit of the documentary. The weather had deteriorated so much that we were confined to camp, so today was perfect for the attempt. We had gone to extraordinary lengths to get a bottle of French bubbly up there. In mountaineering terms it weighed a tonne especially considering we had all cut our toothbrushes in half just to save a few precious grams.

In theory the cork should fly further at altitude. Champagne bottles are pressurised for sea level so at altitude the pressure inside a bottle is far greater, relative to the outside air, causing the cork to explode more violently from the bottle. We hoped to smash the thirty metre mark. Neil sat on the snow gassing to the camera, like a seasoned sports commentator.

'The most important people here today,' he continued, 'are the two participants who are going to actually launch this champagne cork through the extra thin atmosphere we've had specially shipped in: Ballantyne "the corker" and his assistant, Sally "the wench".'

World record attempts like this do not happen spontaneously, they must be filmed from every angle. The crew lugged their equipment down to the other end of our course, where Ballantyne and Sally waited patiently.

Sally was annoyed to be cast as the game-show blonde bimbo and did not take kindly to the suggestion that she act dumb and show off her tits, an impossibility given her three layers of clothing. She pulled the bottle of champagne out from under her fluffy jacket with a half-hearted flurry and passed it to Ballantyne.

Ballantyne studied the champagne with cultured interest. He knew that if any of the guides thought his shoulder injury was too severe he would be banned from going any higher. Whenever he was out of his tent he would avoid drawing attention to his injury by taking his sling off and pretending to be very active. Then he would slip back to his tent to rest. All eyes were on him now. He wore his grey butler's uniform and a starched expression.

'Champagne Louis Roederer, oui,' he muttered, in a phoney French accent. 'Looks like a good popping year... Wind direction fair, here we go...'

Out of camera view, he gave the bottle a good shake and the cork exploded. It flew weakly down the course, landing well short of the intended mark. Neil dived at it, scooped it into his top hat and sprinted past the world record line.

'It's a world record,' he screamed, swinging round to camera.

Everybody dutifully clapped, knowing the whole episode was another cinematic farce. We waited patiently for the next scene. Nothing happened apart from a snowflake which floated erratically towards the ground and unwisely chose to land on Avril's nose. She slapped it irritably, as if it were a horse fly.

Slowly everyone mumbled their excuses and drifted off to the cramped confines of the tents to escape the bad weather. We had a whole day to kill and nothing to do.

I wandered over to Glen's tent to annoy him. As usual, I wanted to put in place overly-elaborate plans in case we failed to reach the summit. Glen was surrounded by piles of camera equipment, intently polishing a lens with a clean cloth. He waited for me to speak.

'Glen, if we don't reach the summit, will you stay back and film a second attempt?'

He glanced up briefly and then acted as if he had not heard me while he thought about his answer. He carefully breathed on his lens cloth to dampen it before removing some minute speck of dust from the glass.

'Don't worry, this dump won't last,' he said, without looking up, referring to the snow fall.

There was a silence. I thought he was going to say something else. He didn't. The conversation was over and I knew he would not stay for a second attempt. It was a day full of pregnant pauses.

If we failed on this attempt only Neil and Trace had agreed to stay behind in Peru for a second climb. I was sure we would be a disastrous trio. Avril promised to stay only if we shot the cook.

Most people thought we were giving it our best shot and if we failed there was no point repeating the attempt. We had already been away nearly five weeks, cut off from family, friends and home comforts. The real world beckoned; a society in which Peru had no significance except as the birthplace of Paddington Bear, a world in which you are not faced with life and death issues every day but with its own share of torment: shopping trolleys which are impossible to manoeuvre because of faulty wheels, adhesive tape which only sticks to your hand, and insistent telephones which drag you out of the shower and then stop ringing when you lift the receiver.

As I wandered to my tent I looked up towards the approximate position of the summit, hidden in thick cloud. Conditions must be horrific on the exposed areas of the mountain. Thank God Milton had overruled our lemming instincts.

The camp was deserted and it was now snowing heavily. I was about to unzip my tent door when I heard Trace giggling inside. I stood listening, then I heard Neil whispering to her. There was more laughter.

I shook my head. What were they playing at now?

My only option was to go and take Neil's place in his tent with Murf and Avril. They welcomed me. Both knew what was happening. Murf lay in his sleeping bag looking dejected. Glen had given him every drug he had to try to control his cough but nothing worked. As Murf moved up the mountain, his cough worsened because of the constant hyperventilation. He knew that the only cure was to leave the mountain.

I sat seriously discussing with Murf whether the conditions would clear for tomorrow's early start. A few tents away in the Huascaran Sheraton, Eddie and Sally were debating the same topic from a very different angle.

'The snow has been fucking dumping down,' Eddie dictated to his tape recorder. 'It is coming down cats, dogs and Peruvian donkeys.'

'According to the Glen school of meteorology,' Sally chipped in, 'the mountain isn't dangerous unless the weather really craps out and dumps. Since we have diagnosed both of these we would like to know what Milton's next move will be at five o'clock tomorrow morning.'

'I think that five o'clock rendezvous is going to be very, very, very, very, very fucking interesting,' Eddie predicted.

203

'But Sally, on to more important things. How is the Tent-Melter Competition coming on?'

Farting is an integral part of high-altitude digestion. Sally had christened a very bad fart a 'tent-melter'.

'After my attempt at the Tent-Melting Medal,' she said, 'you produced a startling, in fact astounding performance which blew away all other previous attempts. Your training has paid off, your effort has paid off, your mental attitude has paid off and I really do think in the Huascaran Tent-Melter's Stakes, Eddie, you are the person to beat.'

Sally and Eddie were very close. Eddie tended towards strong mood swings, one moment loving the expedition, the next talking about giving up. Sally stabilised his moods and he looked after her. He always walked ahead each day, pitched the tent and made sure she had enough food and water.

Two hours later, Jim bellowed through the swirling blizzard to announce that supper was ready. It was musical chairs time. Neil left my tent, poked his head cheerfully into his tent; I glared at him, he avoided eye contact, grabbed his bowl, left his tent and I followed but went to my tent.

It was nearly dark and I noticed the snow was frozen hard underfoot. The temperature had already started its nightly sky dive to minus ten degrees Celsius so tonight was going to be particularly cold. As I unzipped my tent flap, Trace gazed up from her sleeping bag, a lock of blonde hair hung lazily over one eye. She gave me one of her helpless-little-girl looks.

'Can you get some supper for me as well?' she pleaded.

All sorts of replies spun around my head but at this stage of the expedition there seemed little point in making a scene. I took both our plates to collect supper. I scurried back before the food could get cold.

We sat in our tent eating spaghetti in a tense silence. Momentarily I put my bowl down on her sleeping mat and she moved her mat without realising, spilling my food. I stared at the spaghetti congealing on the muddy tent floor, closed my eyes and rubbed my forehead to control my anger.

'Sorry,' I heard her meekly say.

Except for the necessary pleasantries, we never spoke again.

I looked at my watch. Only two-thirty in the morning. Twenty-five minutes had passed since I last looked. I could not remember ever having so much time in which to do nothing.

I buried myself in my sleeping bag again. After four weeks of living in the same bag, the smell was revolting. Like sleeping in a football-club laundry basket. Only worse.

The combined smell of myself and my sleeping bag would have sent most people screaming from the tent. Perversely, I now quite liked the stench. It was a homely smell, my only refuge from the rigours of this masochistic sport. Now I understood how kings, queens and commoners lived with their own body odours during the Middle Ages. Happily they thought washing was unhealthy.

Over the last four weeks we had all become very sensitive to our bodies' warning signals. We looked for signs of dehydration (yellow urine), malnutrition (fatigue), sunstroke (headaches), altitude sickness (debilitating headaches and vomiting), giardia (rotten-egg burps), hypothermia (shivering, followed by narcotic lackadaisical optimism), frostbite (the total numbing of fingers or toes) and exhaustion (extreme lethargy).

I noticed a new and subtle change in my body. I had lost around eight kilos and was thinner than at any other time in my adult life. All my spare fat had long gone. My body was starting to restrict the rate at which it ate away at the small amounts of remaining muscle.

I started to feel the cold severely that night. The chill itself became a chronic condition. Every now and then my internal thermostat would switch on the emergency shivering for fifteen minutes, then shut it off again. For a while I felt slightly better but soon the bitter cold crept back. I began to appreciate what Trace had put up with over the last four weeks; being so thin and small she felt the cold more than anyone.

Another ache arrived which I knew I could not ignore. I needed to go to the toilet. The night was pitch black and in my dozy state I often wasn't sure if I was staring at the inside of the tent or the inside of my eyelids. This pitch darkness could only mean one thing — thick cloud and snow.

I lay in my pongy bag, occasionally shivering, my bladder slowly forcing me to get up. Procrastination was pointless. Like a hole in a shoe when you are walking in the rain, the feeling could only get worse. Reluctantly, I crawled out, in the process disturbing Trace. Outside the tent I carefully walked towards where I thought the crevasse powder room should be.

The darkness was almost complete. I only knew it was snowing because I could feel the flakes hitting my lips. I was worried I would fall into the crevasse before I saw it. I peed anywhere, hoping it was not on my ice axe.

Then the retreat started, a trudge back round the dim outline of the tent, before thankfully wriggling back into my cold sleeping bag, once again disturbing Trace. I lay there shivering, thinking how extraordinary it was watching my body fall apart. I was determined always to remember just how awful I felt at that moment to ensure I never went mountaineering again.

A few tents away Ballantyne also lay awake, no doubt thinking similar thoughts. The cold and his painful shoulder robbed him of any sleep. Strange to think as he suffered, others were about to enjoy fundraising dinners in Australia and England that same night. Ballantyne had been the prime mover behind the formation of the Social

Climbers' official charity support group, The Hangers On Club. It now numbered seven hundred strong. That night fundraising 'thermal' dinner parties were being held in Australia, as well as a special charity dance in London organised by my family. Between England and Australia we eventually raised $30 000 for the National Heart Foundation of Australia and National Heart Hospital in London.

Ballantyne's determination to form the Hangers On Club was part of the same drive that had taken him this far up Huascaran. But the signs of physical deterioration and mental stress were very obvious. His personality had altered and he had become short-tempered and self-centred.

Murf was also under stress because of his continuous cough, but it affected him differently. He needed people to look after him, so he became softer and more approachable.

Sally had changed the most. At the beginning of the expedition she had been as unconfident as Deirdre. Whereas Deirdre had shrunk from the challenge, Sally had grown with it. On Huascaran she was rapidly becoming one of the more confident and supportive team members.

The second lay-day dawned overcast but by ten the sun started burning off the clouds, revealing Huascaran. At last the weather was improving.

We crawled out of our tents. Sally and Neil started organising the morning's entertainment. We set up legless chairs in the snow and sat absorbing the sun. Neil made everyone a cup of tea and Sally and Eddie threw open their larder of jam and biscuits. We sat back and for the first time in two days enjoyed ourselves.

Sally read aloud from the expedition's only book, the mountaineering satire, *The Ascent of Rum Doodle*. Tomorrow we were going to climb the icefall, so Sally chose the appropriate text.

Sir Hugely Havering — Chairman of the Rum Doodle Committee — in 1947, had written: 'The mountain is difficult — severe, even

— but it will go.' Later reconnaissance had questioned whether the icefall itself would go, but the final verdict had been that it would. Sir Hugely himself had summed up the prevailing opinion thus: 'Given team spirit and good porters, the mountain will go.'

But as we stood on the glacier we were awed by the mighty bastion which reared its majestic head against the cloudless sky. In that moment we were humbled by the task we had set ourselves, and I for one sent up a fervent prayer that I would not be found wanting in the ordeal that lay ahead of us. In such moments a man feels close to himself.

We stood there, close to ourselves, until sunset, the supreme artist touched the snowfields of the mighty bastion with a rose-tinted brush and the mountains became a vision such as few eyes have beheld.

Reality intruded when three French climbers and their guides walked into camp, having failed to reach the summit. They spoke of driving blizzards, dangerous crevasses and other mountain horrors. We all listened politely, but I for one believed that it was mostly exaggeration, to justify their failure.

More spiritually-inclined mountaineers would claim the mountain was angry that afternoon. The warm day made large amounts of new snow on the mountain unstable, creating avalanches. They started small, just a distant bang, followed by a mere thousand tonnes of snow cascading down the steep slopes towards us. As the day wore on they grew bigger.

When an avalanche began all conversation stopped. We stared and listened as it gathered momentum, rushing down the mountain before disappearing down one of the three crevasses protecting us from its force.

Late in the afternoon there was a particularly powerful avalanche. It started just below the summit of Huascaran and thundered towards us, jumping the first crevasse without losing strength. The second crevasse slightly weakened its charge but still the enormous cloud of powder snow continued and the roar grew louder.

I watched its approach, ready to hit the snow and make a safe space to breathe in. It died in the third crevasse; only a fine mist of powder snow drifted through camp. The silence was broken by a nervous laugh and then we all continued to do nothing.

It is fortunate that the two biggest killers on a mountain are in a constant battle against one another. The avalanche is neutralised by the crevasse which in turn is plugged by the avalanche.

As the afternoon slipped by we unwisely began to treat the mountain as a playground. Neil found a dustbin liner and started tobogganing down a slope. Soon everyone was joined together in a human toboggan chain and we raced down to the bottom.

Unfortunately, a different type of bottom had also been using the slope. As we wore a groove in the snow we discovered we were sledding through a previous expedition's toilet. Unharmed, except for some minor changes to the colour of our clothes, most of us decided to call it a day. Trace, Neil and Tenzing moved to a relatively untested slope and continued.

Unknowingly, they wakened a hidden monster lying just beneath the snow. Tenzing was half-way down the slope when he broke the surface and started falling into the jaws of a crevasse, without a safety rope.

It was a new crevasse, seeing the light of day for the first time. Only a metre wide and fifteen metres long, it was at least thirty metres deep with completely sheer sides. As the glacier had moved down the mountain, a crack had formed, slowly widening until it broke the surface. Tenzing had caused its premature birth.

He had a fraction of a second to save himself, about as long as it takes to read three words. Once his shoulders fell below the level of the snow, he was as good as dead.

Tenzing had to do two things in that time. Throw his

arms out on either side of him in the hope that the crevasse was narrower than his arm-span. And guess correctly which way the crevasse was running. If he threw out his arms over the thin snow above the line of the crevasse he would simply break through and continue falling.

This was a trick crevasse. Normally they run across the slope but this one was running down. Tenzing had lived most of his life in the mountains and reacted instinctively. He did everything right, falling in only up to his armpits. Fortunately Sebastian De La Crue was close by, grabbed a rope and helped Tenzing out.

Milton was furious. He had a nightmare job keeping us alive while we were climbing, without worrying about us in camp. He called everybody over to look at the crevasse and succeeded in frightening us.

Had it been Neil or Trace falling in, he explained, we would never have seen them again. Even if they had the presence of mind to realise the direction of the crevasse, their natural reaction would have been to grab the edge with both hands rather than throw their arms out. They would have grabbed two handfuls of snow and simply slipped in.

'It is not worth trying to get someone out of a crevasse of this type,' he said, 'It is so bloody deep and the body hits the bottom so hard, it wedges itself into the V-shaped bottom.'

I sat staring down into it. Two smooth vertical walls of ice plunged out of sight into the darkness. Before the expedition we had all laughed off the dangers of mountaineering, but everything we had been told was true. We had been incredibly naive.

It was a timely warning for the hazards to come. The two most dangerous days of the expedition were still ahead of us. I didn't know that they were also going to be the hardest and most important days of my life.

21
HUASCARAN,
THE HARD WAY

It just makes me feel better to yell.

Sally

'Fairly hairy'. That was the technical term for the day's climb.

None of the other mountaineering 'terms', which we never understood but had grown to like, were mentioned. There were no references to 'a piece of shit', 'bomb-proof' or 'you could do it in your bloody sleep'. And no one said 'no worries'.

In *Everest The Hard Way* Chris Bonington described climbing the Everest icefall as 'a medieval assault on a fortress...'

We too faced an arduous climb up an icefall. The name explains one of the potential dangers: ice falling. As the glacier moves down, it cracks and chunks of ice fall off. These chunks range in size from a one-cent piece to a bus. The small change didn't bother us but the buses were a worry.

There were two other lethal items on the menu. Because we were climbing up a gully, any avalanche falling in that area would be funnelled our way, wiping the mountain clean of anyone in its path. That was exactly what had happened to five German climbers the previous year.

The third major danger was falling down a crevasse.

211

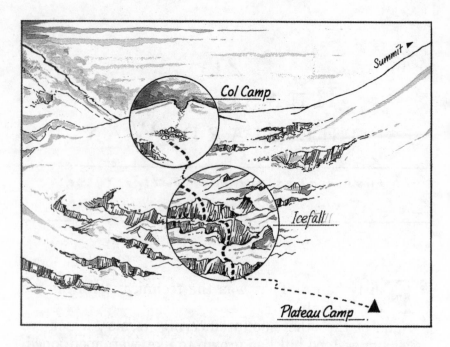

Buckling sheets of ice were constantly opening up crevasses in a series of births. Tenzing's experience the day before could recur anywhere in the icefall. That was why Milton had set up fixed ropes.

In an attempt to reduce these dangers Milton ordered an early start. He wanted to get through the icefall before the sun moved around the mountain and the ice started melting. Yesterday's avalanches had graphically demonstrated the destructive effects of too much sun. Prolonged solar exposure caused the snow and ice to soften and become unstable.

'I'm as nervous as a kitten,' Milton admitted privately.

It was four in the morning. An orange glow was developing on the far side of Huascaran and it was predictably very cold.

I stood outside my tent wiggling my toes inside my boots to keep them warm. Frostbite occurs when the fluids in the cells freeze, causing the cells to expand and the cell walls to

212

rupture. The affected area turns into a glutinous mass of destroyed cells. Severe frostbite can cause gangrene and the affected area may have to be amputated. Contrary to what one would expect, when all the cells are freezing you cannot feel anything because the nerves stop working. It is when the damaged cells thaw out, that the excruciating pain starts.

Since all the nerves at the tips of my toes had already been destroyed, I knew I had to be extra careful. Still wiggling my toes I attached crampons to my boots and gloated about the early start. I had been heavily criticised for my early-morning efforts before the first dinner at Pisco. Now we were heading off even earlier.

There was a different sound in the camp that morning. Something was missing. I looked around in the pre-dawn light, trying to fathom the change. Then I realised we were not being treated to the dulcet tones of Murf's abuse. We had all grown used to his encouragement in the mornings.

'Okay youse miserable bastards, this isn't a boy scouts' picnic,' he'd shout. 'Get ya bloody gear packed. Stop fucking singing, Watson!'

We all secretly liked Murf's sergeant-major behaviour. It was as much a part of the expedition as being ill. Unfortunately that was now his problem. He described his misery in his diary.

I felt like a piece of shit this morning. As soon as I got out of the cold tent my cough became unbearable. I decided to wait in my bag until the day warmed up a bit. Breakfast was disgusting as usual — two mouthfuls of cold porridge.

The documentary crew came over to interview me. I felt very nervous, a bit desperate and looked my usual mess. Greasy hair stuck out in every direction from under my red duvet jacket. My red scarf was untidily coiled around my neck. Two white circles around my eyes indicated where my dark glasses had shielded the sun and made me look like a startled owl. I put on my Ansett cap and slipped into press-agent mode.

'It is so cold I can hardly feel my hands,' I muttered, pushing my sleeping bag into my pack. 'This is our one big chance for the summit. If the weather holds I think some of us will definitely make it. We have almost run out of time, energy, fuel and food. We've got to get up there. We've got to erect the dining-room table and we've got to have the bloody dinner party.'

I threw my pack on to my back and started off. The first section for the day was the walk to the base of the icefall, a relatively easy hike up a gentle slope.

After three days' rest at Plateau Camp, I felt stronger than at any other time on the expedition and my knee was much better. I immediately overtook Ballantyne and soon Trace's purple pack came within my sights, loaded to the hilt. On top of her normal load she carried a chair, four detachable legs, a tent and the orchid flower arrangement, all strapped to the outside of her pack. Since the pack was moving up the mountain I could only assume Trace was under the enormous load somewhere. As I drew closer I saw her skinny legs, struggling through the deep snow.

I trudged ten metres behind her, stopping whenever she did, positioning myself in her slipstream. Then I pulled out and accelerated to overtake, probably reaching the reckless speed of one and a half kilometres per hour. Just to rub it in, I managed to gasp a 'hello' to her as I 'sprinted' past. The Goddess at Altitude ignored me.

It was the high point of my day. I kept the pressure up and was delighted to find I was widening the gap. How long could I keep up this pace?

Back at camp Murf had seriously underestimated the extent of his illness. He was the last to leave, walking with Jim. But for Murf's continuous cough, they would have caught up without any trouble. Now, the greater the exertion, the more he coughed. After one particularly savage bout, he looked down and saw bright red specks in the snow. He had begun to cough up blood and should have turned back. But he chose to continue. He was carrying the stove and the stove was essential for the success of the expedition.

I reached the bottom of the first of three ice walls in the icefall. I looked at it with alarm. It was twice the height of Pisco's ice wall and much steeper.

Halfway up I ran out of energy, my arms and legs went limp and I hung by my harness like a corpse from a rope. My race with Trace, though satisfying, had drained precious energy. Lethargically I glanced down the cliff and saw Tenzing staring up at me.

'You okay?' he shouted.

I waved weakly with my ice axe to show that I could still move.

'Jolly good,' he shouted, flashing a warm smile. His friendly concern made me feel better immediately.

Ballantyne was next up the wall. His shoulder was so heavily strapped he could hardly use it. He didn't look left or right, he didn't smile or talk, he just focused totally on the job in hand. I suddenly realised he was going to prove us all wrong and get to the summit. At the top of the wall he slumped sideways on his good shoulder and lay on his pack, gasping for breath and staring at the sky.

The documentary crew were filming at the top of the ice wall. Neil was the next up the wall, in typically masochistic fashion, he enjoyed it.

> Climbing the ice wall was one of the high points so far. It was like running a marathon in the most beautiful place in the world. I teetered on the wall, balancing on my crampons and ice axe and gazing at the mountains stretching away for miles and miles. The adrenalin was pumping, it was so hard, it was glorious. I thought, yes, this is what I've come for.

Sally followed Neil up the wall and took a different view.

She was annoyed that she was continuously being asked to stop and hang from the rope halfway up the wall so the camera crew could film Neil.

'Will the fucking film crew ... just let us get on with it!' she shouted, with a desperate edge to her voice.

Neil turned around and insisted they were only doing their job, which was to film him.

'It just makes me feel better to yell,' she shouted back.

Avril collapsed at the top of the ice wall. She knelt submerged under her red duvet jacket, her forehead pressed on the snow, gasping for air. As if she was facing Mecca in prayer. In my own exhausted haze I realised that she was finally discovering what she had travelled round the world to find. She was facing the barriers of her own physical limitations. I just hoped she was able to dig deep and reach beyond.

The camera feverishly recorded the Social Climbers falling apart. But they missed the real drama below. Murf documented his progress.

> I got halfway up to the ice wall, then I had another vicious coughing attack. I bent over double and lay on the snow. As I stared at my blood in the snow a few inches away from my face I knew I was at a crossroad. Jim waited for me to recover and then asked if I wanted to continue.
>
> I've never been a mad summit person. I have enjoyed seeing South America and training a bunch of no-hopers to a standard where some of them have a chance of getting to the summit. I could have carried on and made myself a liability for everyone else or turned back. I decided to turn around. I gave my stove to Jim and started walking down the mountain.

We were all shocked when Jim reached the top of the ice wall and told us Murf had turned back. It had never occurred to me that Murf would not summit and it proved there was a lot of luck in mountaineering. He was diagnosed later as having bronchitis. Any one of us could have been afflicted.

Two Social Climbers down. Only one to go.

If, like Murf, I had a wife and baby, I might have given up just at the *sight* of the heart of the icefall. Even a bushman from the Kalahari Desert would have sensed its treachery. It was the kind of place one creeps through for fear of waking it up. Enormous blocks of ice, haphazardly piled on top of each other, flanked us as we struggled up narrow gullies. Small crevasses, only a few centimetres wide, criss-crossed the gullies.

As usual, we were late. The sun had swung around the mountain and now glinted off the tops of the ice battlements around us, causing them to soften. Soon the snow would melt and chunks could start to fall. The gullies were littered with lumps of ice from recent collapses. No one talked, no one stopped. We hurried through as fast as possible.

After two hours, I followed Eddie up the last wall. As he climbed out of the sullen icefall the sun started to catch the fragments of ice which he had dislodged with his ice axe. It looked like an asteroid storm falling towards me.

At the top of the icefall we all felt a great sense of relief, although Murf's departure had punctured morale. Neil, Sally, Trace, Avril and I stopped for a drink. Milton lumbered towards us and I fully expected him to walk straight past. He stopped, dropped his enormous pack and sat down heavily on the snow.

'I'm fucking knackered.'

It was music to our ears. At last a superhuman mountaineer had admitted to exhaustion. I think Milton realised that when Murf dropped out it rocked our confidence. By admitting he too was finding it hard, he actually encouraged us. We felt more like equals.

I also believe Milton was proud of us. He had taken on the

project over eighteen months ago and worked with great enthusiasm when most other mountaineers would not consider it. He was still the strength behind the team. We sat together above the icefall on a sunny day at 5700 metres, sharing three tins of condensed milk.

The lower range of the Andes was spread out in front of us. No snow covered this dark brown section. Small puffy clouds scurried away from us over the mountains, like cotton-wool airships.

Sally summed up the atmosphere of our little gathering.

We just sat back slurping our condensed milk and farting. We felt no pressure.

Inevitably the conversation turned to Murf. There were several schools of thought about his decision to turn back. Everybody claimed they had predicted it. Most people enjoyed the notion they would make a good detective. Some were suspicious of how badly he wanted to make it. Neil said he would have continued in Murf's condition. He was not boasting, he was just saying that nothing would stop him from reaching the summit.

It was Milton who pointed out the difference between the obsessive behaviour of Neil, Ballantyne and me, and that of a sensible mountaineer like Murf.

'I admire someone who knows his capabilities,' he said. 'Murf will live to an old age and enjoy the mountains. You can't enjoy the mountains if you are dead.'

After half an hour we set off up towards the col once more, not realising we were being watched from below. Murf sat despondently in Plateau Camp, coughing and staring up at us. Later, he wrote his black thoughts on that day.

I got back to camp and there was nothing to eat, I watched the last few stragglers getting safely up and I was happy for them.
I'm not disappointed with myself but annoyed because I've been

cheated of a chance of the summit by bad food. Three stoves isn't
adequate, there aren't enough tents and the hygiene is terrible.

We arrived at the Col Camp, which paradoxically, was
not in the col. The camp was a series of terraces cut out of
the slope below the col. The scene in camp would have made
a warthog blush as we sat eating our last supper. Empty
tins of tuna lay strewn on the snow, soup was spilt over
duvet jackets in the rush to finish one bowl and gulp a
second. It was like a panic buy before a petrol strike. The
energy we extracted from this supper was critical for each
of us, if we were to have a chance of getting to the summit
tomorrow.

Both Ballantyne and Avril were exhausted and had gone
to bed early. Trace moved into the Huascaran Sheraton
with Sally and Eddie. Trace lightheartedly recorded her
thoughts before the final summit bid.

> *Chris was avoiding me like no one's business today. I found him a*
> *bit irritating this morning and I rather snapped at him. On the*
> *way up, whenever I stopped, he stopped just short of me so we*
> *didn't have to talk.*
>
> *He's now sharing a tent with Nicholas — the tent of the lonely*
> *men. No doubt they are having a very serious talk about the*
> *summit bid. Tomorrow I'm going to be extremely selfish. No one is*
> *having any of my Cadbury's Eggs, I'm having them all myself.*
> *You can fuck the team player.*

22
IT'S MY PARTY AND I'LL DIE IF I WANT TO

It wasn't a work of art, it was a work of desperation.

Glen

The combination of the cold, the rarefied oxygen at 6200 metres, the wind and our nerves stopped everyone from sleeping. Sally described it.

> The night was wild. The wind knocked the tent around like a troop of abominable snowmen throwing snowballs at us. I lay awake all night listening to Trace and Eddie breathing, feeling frozen even with all my clothes on. For the first time on the expedition I was truly frightened.

Avril and Neil stayed up all night massaging each other's feet and nestling them in each other's armpits to stave off frostbite. The rest of us lay in our tents, like soldiers before a battle, waiting for dawn.

We had been ordered to go to the toilet right beside our tents because the camp was perched on the edge of a steep slope leading to a set of crevasses. If anyone slipped in the dark they wouldn't stand much chance.

Life had become very simple. In the group we had an accountant, an actor, a computer analyst, a lawyer, a stuntgirl, a travel agent and a waiter. It did not matter what we each had done in our lives or would do in the future, the only issue was who would have the mental and

220

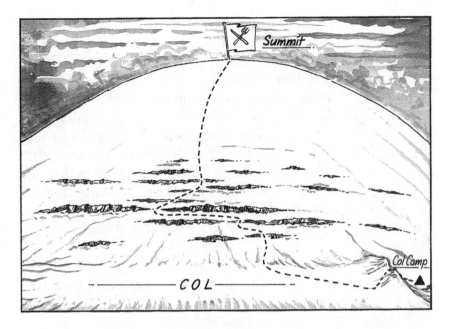

physical energy to reach the summit.

By the morning, Neil had lost his normal hyperactive bounce and his documentary grin. 'There are seven Social Climbers left,' he said to the camera. 'I wonder if any of us will sip the Hardy's wine on the summit.'

Little did he know none of us would.

I looked up at the mountain. The sky was clear but there was a plume of snow spewing off the top, indicating strong winds. Down at Plateau Camp, Murf wrote his last diary entry of the expedition.

> They don't have a hope. The weather has robbed them of a chance. I'm heading down to Musho now. You get to a point when you have either climbed the mountain or it has beaten you and you have to say, 'I'm going home'. I'm relieved it is all over.

Even on this, our most important day, the Social Climbers were late. It was not a good start given that today was a race against time. This was one party I did not want to miss. I knew I was slow so I packed my thermal black tie, some dining equipment, survival clothes, a tin of condensed milk, three litres of water and my Louis XIV chair and started climbing. Only Ballantyne, Jim and the documentary team were in front of me.

Jim helped me across a crevasse on to the col. I had never encountered such ferocious conditions. A sixty kilometre wind funnelled between the north and south peaks, blasting a mass of swirling snow and ice along the col with enough force to blow you off your feet. For the first time on the expedition Chris Hilton and Glen actually looked excited, like a couple of playful huskies (Photo 43).

'This is like the Antarctic,' Glen screamed cheerfully in my ear.

'Very good, er, thanks Glen... remind me never to go there.' I staggered off, wondering how he found pleasure standing in a wind tunnel while little pieces of ice ripped him apart. I never did understand mountaineers.

Approaching the second crevasse the three porters passed me, moving powerfully up the mountain under their enormous packs.

'Hola, Darwil,' they shouted cheerfully.

'Hombres Supers,' I muttered under my breath. At least they were being paid to put up with this.

There were two basic sections on Huascaran, neither worth getting out of a sleeping bag to climb. Section one comprised three crevasses and five ice walls, difficult but protected from the wind. Above that was the dome which was certain to be a long snow slog. Here the wind would be at its most ferocious and here most people would fail.

I was constantly hyperventilating, taking about one step for every three breaths. Gradually I caught up with Ballantyne and asked how he was coping. His woollen hat almost totally covered his dark glasses and his whole body looked limp under his enormous blue duvet jacket. It was going to be a long day and he looked exhausted already.

Pausing to try and catch his breath he gasped a reply.

'It's just up... and bloody... up.' He was obviously in pain.

We had been told that above 5300 metres the conditions became harder very quickly because the oxygen levels drop off rapidly and we were now one thousand metres above that mark. Already today felt much harder than yesterday. Milton was the last to leave the camp.

I looked up and couldn't believe it. Everyone was going up the mountain like blue-arsed flies. I was very proud — the Social Climbers were moving like experienced mountaineers.

Sebastian and Tenzing performed like the world-class mountaineers they were. At each fifty-degree ice wall they climbed up, secured the ropes and went on to organise the next. There was a sense of urgency. Everybody knew we were running out of time.

Eddie and Trace were flying. Neil was once again his normal excited self. Having climbed each ice wall, most of us were reduced to lying on our backs exhausted, feeling like death. The greatest armchair mountaineer the world has ever seen would appear over the edge grinning from ear to ear, ranting and raving, his toy koala still clinging defiantly to the rim of his top hat.

'This is fantastic... we love it. What a view... what a day... what a sport. Too much of this... is barely enough, great... We've got to do more of this, Chris.' (Photo 44)

He was right about one thing. It was beautiful. We were hundreds of metres above all the other mountains and the visibility was exceptional. The whole of the Andes was laid out in front of us. Far below we could just pick out Pisco. It was hard to believe that only ten days ago we had struggled to climb what now seemed to be a minor peak.

Yet as we continued up everybody sank within themselves. I was also very aware that the doco crew were holding people up, as they had done with Sally yesterday. I insisted that Glen and Chris stop doing so.

'Look, Chris, I'm here to do a job... and you are not going

to stop me,' Glen snapped. 'Why don't you concentrate your energies... on getting up the mountain.' I didn't want an argument. I didn't have the energy. I let it go. Glen described the atmosphere.

> *I realised then how strained the Social Climbers were, both physically and mentally. Chris was particularly stressed. Neil actually shut up for the first time on the expedition. I knew there was something going on in their brains.*

By now we had crossed three crevasses and climbed four ice walls. It was already midday and we had been climbing for three hours. As the ice wall gave way to the dome section of Huascaran we passed a series of phallic ice structures. I photographed each Social Climber being buffeted by the wind as they struggled through the maze (Photo 45).

By the time I put my camera away I realised to my horror I was at the back. The lead I so badly needed had gone. Ballantyne was the only one behind me. I waited for him to catch up.

'Every time... somebody overtakes me... I lose my rhythm,' he complained. He was in trouble so I took some of his load.

We both needed to speed up. I knew at this rate we would never make it. It would be dark in five hours and we could not possibly descend in the dark.

It is hard to express what it is like walking at that altitude. Tim Macartney-Snape compared it to 'running a marathon with a hangover', but to me it was just fucking awful. Ballantyne and I settled into a mind-numbing routine. Three breaths, one step, three breaths, one step, ten steps then a rest, ten steps then a rest, all the time staring at the snow a metre in front of us, just concentrating on keeping our feet moving.

We gasped for air at a frantic rate, never seeming able to extract enough oxygen from the thin atmosphere. The physical conditions would have been unbearable had I not been in an exhausted daze the whole time. Our bodies mercifully diverted blood away from the brain to the muscles and vital organs, making anything other than basic thinking near impossible. I did however make a mental note never to forget all the other promises I had made never to go mountaineering again.

We only had two more crevasses to cross. I reached the first and in a semi-conscious state noticed two snow bridges spanning it. Ignoring where most of the footprints led, I staggered over to the furthest bridge. As I neared it I noticed a luminous blue effect in the footprints on the bridge. I concluded that the snow was so thin, the light was shining up through the bridge.

To cross the bridge would effectively be committing suicide. But I did not care any more. In my dazed state, I was dimly aware I was not going to make it to the summit. But I knew I could never turn back. So I started crossing the bridge.

I placed my foot into the luminous blue footprint, expecting to experience the sickening feeling of the delicate structure collapsing. It did not. I lumbered across and stopped on the far side, a little confused. Then I realised the luminous effect had been caused by the light hitting the footprints at a certain angle. For the first time that day I smiled.

Once out of the shelter of the gullies we were exposed to the full force of the wind again and the temperature plummeted. Intermittent flurries of powder snow blew across the bleak snowfields. The landscape was totally featureless, just white snow and blue sky. I could see clouds foaming up below us like a pan of milk about to boil over, only the tops of the surrounding mountains were still visible above the clouds. In my dopey state I totally missed the significance of this.

Now I could understand why most people give up on this section. It never seemed to end. Every time we reached what I thought must be the summit we discovered another summit ahead.

The only targets we had to aim at were four specks of colour in the distance, two stationary and two moving. The green and blue specks were Milton and Britannion waiting for us; Avril and Sally, both wearing red, were moving up the mountain. Neil, Eddie and Trace had already disappeared ahead. I swore at Neil, perhaps unfairly. It was unlike him not to help the weaker climbers.

Everyone knew it was a race. If you were not there for the dinner party you missed out. And we were getting further and further behind. Ballantyne stopped again. I gave both of us the mountain equivalent of a line of cocaine, opening a tin of condensed milk and forcing him to eat some with me. If this did not get us going, nothing would. The high sugar content always produced startling effects on my energy levels. I took the rest of the kit from his pack and we staggered on.

Finally we caught up to Milton and Britannion. They stood with their backs to the wind, their heads completely covered by their jacket hoods. Ballantyne slumped down. My insides were in a terrible state and I suddenly needed to go to the toilet. I retched at the diarrhoea.

Trace was the first Social Climber to reach the summit. There is no doubt she was an exceptional athlete. She bounced around looking like a multicoloured Michelin Man, kissing everything that wasn't snow.

I was really proud of keeping up with Tenzing who goes like a steam train. When I got to the top I instantly burst into tears. It was so emotional and I thought, 'Here I am standing on the top of the world and I'm crying and I cannot believe it, I'm so happy'.

I was waving my ice axe around and jumping up and down. The sun was out at that point and I could see all the other peaks. Neil was the next up and I started shouting at him, 'Come on, you

226

can do it,' I burst into tears again when he arrived. We hugged
and he started to cry too.

Down the mountain, Milton could see Ballantyne was in a bad way.

'Ballantyne,' he shouted above the noise of the wind, 'it is still... a long way to the summit. I'm sure you could... make it, but getting down will be... dangerous.'

I could not really see Ballantyne's face. It was obscured by his hat, duvet jacket hood and dark glasses. However I could tell by the way he sat stooped over in the snow hyperventilating, that he was beaten.

I think for the first time he had to admit something which he had always ignored. At sixty-two he was getting no younger. We were less than three hundred metres from the summit but he knew that short distance at this altitude was the equivalent of several kilometres at sea level. Without looking up he admitted defeat.

'This's... the end... for me.'

It was the saddest moment of the expedition. He was the one who most deserved to stand on the summit. Ballantyne had sustained the greatest pain, had looked after people when they were down and had helped keep morale up by being entertaining. He had come within three hundred metres of achieving a lifelong ambition but that chance would never come again. Britannion took him down.

Milton then turned to me. 'Chris you should... go down too,' he shouted.

It took a second for the full significance of this to sink in. I suddenly realised I was about to fail. It panicked me and I point-blank refused. Milton described my condition.

You can tell by looking at a person their levels of exhaustion. The
way they talk, blink, move their hands, and Chris was totally
stuffed. I knew he was determined to get to the top so I thought
there would be one person who might have to be rescued.

227

Milton suggested I climb in front of him. I realised he was testing me. The wind was so strong, the snow drifted back onto our tracks as if the mountain was trying to eradicate any evidence of our invasion. Every time I put my foot down I sank into the snow half-way up to my knee, then moved forward and had to pull my foot out. Milton therefore had a clean imprint to step into, making it easier. He wanted to see if I could keep going at the front.

In exercise, the brain is the limiting factor rather than the body. The brain will keep whispering to you, 'You are totally exhausted, slow down,' when in fact it knows the body has heaps of energy left. Anybody who has been in a life-threatening situation will know this is true.

The half-tin of condensed milk had done wonders and I started flying up the mountain. Avril and Sally came in sight again, I was catching them. Milton was now satisfied I would make it, and passed me.

I followed behind him, fixated on his right boot. It had what looked like a daub of brown paint at the heel. The speck got smaller and smaller and then disappeared. I stopped, surprised and looked up to see that he had moved ahead of me. I was at the back again.

Lethargically, I gazed around. It was then I noticed the first wispy clouds racing across the snow fields. The cloud level was rising up around the mountain. I took a swig of water and watched the horrifying transformation. The sunlight started to flicker as the clouds hurried overhead. Finally the sun disappeared, it started to blizzard and the temperature fell further. Within fifteen minutes what had previously been just a desperately unpleasant place deteriorated into one of the most dangerous environments on earth.

Even with my limited mountaineering experience I knew we were in deep trouble. There were two options. Either they were having the dinner party without me or they would cancel it and start coming down. I hoped they chose the former. It would be too dangerous coming down in the dark and in these conditions we could not stay up there. As with most of my mountaineering predictions I was wrong. I started trudging up again.

I could still just see Sally and Avril on the brow of the next rise. They looked like two mechanical red blobs. Both stooped over, they walked in file, their legs moving in time as if tied together. Sally described her ordeal.

> It was the hardest day of my life but I felt that I owed it to the whole group to make it. I was exhausted from the beginning. I kept saying, 'Avril, where is the... summit? It has... to be soon.' Each time we got to the top of a ridge, there were still acres of snow in front of us. The wind was frustrating me and I could never catch my breath.
>
> I was getting very dehydrated. We were supposed to be drinking three litres of water during the day and I had only drunk one. But I couldn't be buggered stopping. It was a twenty-minute rigmarole, breaking the rhythm, getting the pack off, digging around to find the water bottle, having the drink, and then farting around putting it all back. It doesn't sound complicated but at that altitude it is hard to motivate yourself to do anything.
>
> To stop myself thinking how bloody awful it was, I tried to picture something else. I thought about owning a corporate empire and driving a Ferrari but it was too much effort. It was all I could do to let my feet walk without my brain.

Down the mountain I used more bitter thoughts to keep myself motivated. Love and hate are the two strongest emotions and right now I needed to tap into both to keep me going. I thought about Cointreau. How I would love to see their PR agents in this horrific sub-zero environment and watch them flailing around in their low-cut dresses. Their cold controlled exteriors would start breaking down in terror as they realised they couldn't handle it, just like I could not handle the Sydney sponsorship scene.

This stopped me thinking about my exhaustion. I

thought about Trace, her great sense of fun and her wildness, which are so rare. I convinced myself I was doing this for her. I thought about Neil, who always supported me through all my moods, and my family who had encouraged my unusual projects.

Suddenly I woke to reality. Someone was shouting. I knew I must be near the summit. Tenzing came down the mountain towards me. He looked fresh, smiled and offered to take my pack. I refused. I was absolutely stuffed but I had to do it myself.

Finally I saw the summit through the driving snow. Tenzing and Lorenzo had built a short ditch for everyone to huddle in to escape the weather. Chris Hilton and Glen were standing in the blizzard interviewing Neil.

For most people enthusiasm is a personality trait only evident when everything is going just right. It is a basic part of Neil's character. It was obvious he was exhausted, he slurred his words and looked drunk, but still he was grinning.

'To be on the top of Huascaran . . . after so much preparation . . . is absolutely fantastic. I was in tears when I first arrived . . . it is an unbelievable feeling. Now we have got the serious bit . . . otherwise we will never hear the end of it . . . from Darwin. Hopefully no one will get frostbite. My nose is running . . . sorry Mum, if you saw that.'

Everyone, except Sally, cried when they reached the summit. She sat in the snow, the wind inflating her violent pink dress and making her look enormous. She felt so awful all her emotion had been drained, as she explained for the documentary.

'My lungs are . . . about to jump . . . out of . . . my rib cage. I feel sick, dizzy, but it is . . . worth it, being here. Now I just want . . . to get it over . . . and get out of here.'

As I reached the summit Trace hugged me and started to cry again. She looked so happy and unaffected by the altitude and exertion. I tried to tell her about Ballantyne but no sound came out. My vocal cords had given up again. I felt tears welling up for him.

I felt neither happy nor sad but drugged and dazed. I did not even experience that Douglas Adams 'profound feeling of something or other'. I was worried. The ordeal was not over. It was four in the afternoon. We had to have the dinner but the blizzard was getting worse by the minute and the wind felt like it was scything through our clothes. Allowing for wind chill the temperature was minus twenty degrees Celsius and we would never make it down before dark. We were, as Glen would say, 'in deep shit and I mean deep shit'.

Milton insisted we take no more than forty-five minutes for the dinner party. As Tenzing, Jim and Eddie arranged the table we all struggled with our black ties and ball dresses. Our formal wear was designed by Grace Bros to withstand temperatures down to minus twenty degrees Celsius but as night approached the temperature slid further to minus thirty-seven. Visibility decreased to fifty metres and we disappeared into swirling clouds.

Everyone started shivering. Neil decided there was probably a waiver in Debrett's stating that in the event of frostbite, ladies were permitted to wear a jacket at the dinner table. They were exceedingly grateful.

Over a year before I had predicted what the dinner would look like in the expedition prospectus. In retrospect I was a little naive.

> *The luncheon will not be a hurried, dehydrated picnic. It will be a black-tie, three-course, gourmet banquet waited upon by Ballantyne and washed down with champagne. The Louis XIV table will look magnificent and will have all the trappings of a royal visit. While the Social Climbers enjoy the staggering view, Ballantyne will stagger around the table serving the guests.*

The reality was very different. It was both hurried and dehydrated, and to have called it a picnic would have made it sound too smart. It looked more like an outdoor chimney sweeps' convention in the dead of winter.

Our top hats were crumpled, the girls resembled triple-layered piles of duvet jackets draped over chairs, there was no champagne and no Ballantyne to serve it. More spectacular panoramas could be found sitting inside a large refrigerator. The blizzard had created a total white-out.

It was a pathetic sight. Most of the chairs had only a couple of legs and had to be propped up with ice axes and packs. There was little cutlery on the table. Glasses swayed as the wind threatened to rip off the velcro holding them to the tablecloth. They were empty anyway because the Hardy's wine had frozen solid.

Our flowers looked like they had been napalmed and the specially prepared Ansett first-class food had been mistakenly eaten by the porters. A frozen tin of pickled onions and a tin of tuna made poor substitutes, shovelled unceremoniously on six plates. Neil tried to eat but with his first chomp he bit the plastic imitation silver fork in half without making any impression on the frozen tuna.

A few minor aesthetic compromises were the least of our problems. Slowly the humour dawned on me. It was very black. Here we were having a dinner party on the summit of the seventh highest mountain in the world outside the Himalayas, dressed to the nines and getting hypothermia. It was easily the most ridiculous thing we had ever done or would ever do in our lives.

The great irony of the expedition was that the women looked so miserable. The Social Climbers had grown out of the ashes of the Dining Out Club, a group formed with the sole purpose of entertaining women by holding dinners in bizarre locations. Yet on this, our most ambitious venture, we totally failed on the basic premise. The women were neither impressed nor amused. Like us they wanted to get out of there as soon as possible.

We only had fifteen minutes left to film this culinary travesty. The documentary cameras rolled and the curtain went up on the Social Climbers' swansong. My chair had no legs so I stood up to speak from the snow. I looked terrible: lips white with congealed saliva, hat covered with snow, nose guard flapping in the blizzard. I lifted my empty glass and proposed a toast.

'I wish to propose a toast to Ballantyne,' I slurred. 'He got very close... very determined... very sad. Also to Murf, who trained us. We are all... very sad they are not here.'

It was unintentional but I had forgotten Deirdre. 'We have booked Everest for 1993,' I joked, 'for the highest... formal luncheon party.'

'Can you organise... central heating and a... cable car next time?' Neil asked. His condition was rapidly deteriorating. He refused to stand up because he claimed there was a crevasse opening underneath him. In fact he was getting hypothermia.

'I am sure everybody echoes my thoughts,' he said. 'I think... we are all crazy, but I've had the... best time and the... best eighteen months helping you, Chris. This is something... that we will remember for the... rest of our lives. The most important thing is... we are with friends. Thank you, Darwin, from the bottom of my heart. To Chris Darwin, an exceptional man.'

Everybody drank from their empty glasses. I wanted to say one more thing.

'Thank you all very much.' Christ, I meant it. 'You all made this thing happen. Everybody worked incredibly hard. Eddie... was full-time... Avril was working away... Sally was chasing the food... Trace was slogging away and had to... put up with me. Neil, fantastic work.'

I knew I had behaved badly at times and others had not behaved nearly as well as they would have liked. That's what happens on mountains. I wanted them to know I

233

didn't care about the disagreements and selfishness. I just appreciated what everyone had done. I finished in the only possible way.

'And now... I'm getting the fuck... out of here!'

'Joy, joy,' everyone shouted.

'McDonald's... here I come,' slurred Neil.

Everyone left the table. It looked a desolate sight with the tablecloth and flowers flapping in the blizzard and chairs lying broken on the ground. But we had done it.

It is hard to imagine an achievement more fundamentally pointless and more utterly satisfying. Not only had we hosted the world's highest dinner party at 6768 metres, it was also the world's coldest dinner party at minus thirty-seven degrees Celsius, the world's shortest dinner party at about ten minutes' duration, the world's driest dinner party because there was nothing to drink, and quite possibly the dinner party with the most world records. As Glen recalled, the records were the last things we were thinking about.

> *It was a joke. The only thing on everyone's mind was we had to get out of there alive. It wasn't a work of art, it was a work of desperation.*

I had a vague feeling we were about to put another chapter into Milton's book of epic retreats. Having heard about his other escapes this should have made me feel very uneasy. But it didn't, my condition was rapidly deteriorating.

We changed, dismantled the table and threw everything into our packs and started down at high speed. Conditions could not have been worse. Only the guides had thought to bring torches, yet we still had five crevasses to cross in pitch darkness.

Trouble started immediately. Sally said nothing during the dinner and sat at the table with her face hidden under her jacket. In true style she suffered in silence but later made it clear how terrible she had felt.

I was frozen to the core. It was the same feeling as I had on the top of Pisco when I nearly got frostbite and I knew it was serious. I yelled, 'I'm cold, I'm cold I need someone's armpits to put my hands in'.

Jim Nixon obliged.

Hypothermia has three main stages. The first is shivering. The second starts when the body temperature drops below thirty-five degrees Celsius, your heart slows down and you stop shivering. This stage is like a narcotic drug, you cannot co-ordinate your actions and become lethargic. From stage two you can quickly slip into the third stage, which is death. Neil and I both felt drunk, which was strange because neither of us had drunk anything. Another symptom which Glen recognised.

Neil came undone, he dropped his bundle. He was staring square in the face of hypothermia. He kept saying 'Just leave me, I'm fucked'. We ignored that and kept encouraging him, 'Keep going, keep going, keep walking down'.

Neil recalled his dangerous state.

From the time I got up from the table I was in a total daze and drunken state. I got very cold and tired. I think it was also an emotional thing; Chris and I had been working on this for a long time.

One side of my brain was saying, 'Neil you are getting hypothermia, get down off the mountain and get warm'. The other side was whispering, 'Okay, you have done it, relax, isn't this drowsiness blissful? Isn't this a beautiful place? Just sit down and take a bit of a rest and enjoy it.'

I might remember that when I'm coming to the end of my days. I will walk up a mountain, sit down and just let it happen.

Neil, Sally and I were now hardly capable of walking due to exhaustion, various levels of hypothermia and the blizzard. Every few steps I collapsed. Eventually I gave up, sat down and used my legs to pull myself down. Everyone shouted at me to get up immediately. I did and fell over again. In my dazed state I found all this mildly amusing and couldn't understand why they were being so serious.

Glen thought this was the mountain's revenge.

> The mountain let them get away with the dinner at Pisco but now it was reminding them who was boss. There they were, a bunch of beginners climbing down a mountain at night over crevasses in a blizzard, it was potentially lethal. The Social Climbers were scared and humbled.

With the benefit of hindsight I now understand why experienced mountaineers make what appear to be bad decisions and die as a result of them. The mountains are dangerous but more importantly as you get exhausted and hypothermic, you no longer care. But for Jim looking after me, I have little doubt I would have walked straight into a crevasse with a broad grin on my face.

People have criticised Milton for some aspects of the expedition. But no one could criticise his safety standards. Three out of the six Social Climbers were in a very bad way and had to abseil down ice walls and negotiate crevasses in total darkness. Milton walked in step behind Neil ready to grab him each time he fell. Tenzing and Sebastian showed why they were probably two of the best mountaineers in South America. They went in relay down the mountain setting up abseils for us.

Ballantyne was in his sleeping bag 600 metres below being buffeted by the wind. Days later he wrote of his internal torment.

> I've had many setbacks in my life, but few have affected me as much as being chased off Huascaran. I was so bloody determined to make it. The worst part of the whole expedition was lying in the tent waiting for everyone to return. I didn't have a torch or watch.

I was exhausted and my brain started playing havoc with my imagination. I pictured all sorts of accidents: people falling down crevasses, hypothermia or someone being so exhausted that they would simply choose to stay on the mountain. I lay there waiting and fearing the worst.

The men were performing worse than the women. More of the women had reached the summit, they reached it more quickly and now they were not as badly affected by hypothermia. Sally was struggling more than the other women.

I lost Avril on the way down. I started yelling out. It was like one of those nightmares when you try and scream and cannot. I felt the noise was being dissolved by the blizzard. Finally I saw a red blob in the swirling clouds and I caught up with her.

We both seemed to be collapsing and swearing and getting up and collapsing. It was an effort to fall down. Getting up wouldn't have been too hard but for our Frankenstein footwear. I was too exhausted to be frightened, I couldn't care if it was dangerous. I forced myself to say my name and address to see if I was there or not.

We had to do the final abseil down in pitch darkness. Because the rope was very long and the wind so strong we were never sure when the last person was off the rope. We kept shouting down, 'Offfffff rope?' There would be a pause and we would hear the muffled answer coming back up out of the darkness. 'Oteiuifieeee.' We'd say, 'I think that means no'.

Eventually Trace, Chris and I abseiled down on to the col. Trace and Chris were still annoyed with each other and started arguing where the last crevasse was. Trace seemed to know where she was going so I followed her. We could hardly see anything, just snow for forty metres then clouds rushing through the col. All the footprints had been blown away. It was like no-man's-land. We walked towards where we thought the crevasse was, guided by the wind direction. Suddenly I saw a torch ahead. It was Jim.

Half an hour later we entered camp. At last I felt the euphoria

237

the others had experienced on the summit. I felt like a hero returning home from battle.

I will never know how we didn't lose anyone. After the two-hour evacuation everyone was back in camp. Ballantyne was extremely relieved to see us safe and sound.

Neil and Chris were in a strange daze. They had obviously been in serious danger and it was as if they had seen through 'the door'.

We all crawled into our sleeping bags. Most of us didn't sleep that night, we were too cold. Avril stayed up all night massaging Neil to get him warm. It had been the longest day for the Social Climbers.

The red wine thawed rapidly in the warm sun next morning. From inside my tent I heard the cork being pulled, followed by cheers — the guides were celebrating.

Poking my head out, the scene at Col Camp hardly seemed recognisable as the same place as yesterday. The sun shone benignly in the still air. The guides were drinking while the documentary crew filmed Ballantyne re-enacting the moment when he abandoned his summit attempt. The few Social Climbers who were up sat in front of their tents, seemingly shell-shocked. Tenzing hurried around camp grinning and making everyone tea and porridge.

It took me an hour to pack, sorting out my possessions and thoughts. By the time I had finished, my Macpac bulged with gear and my head was clear. I now realised why I felt no elation. I had never doubted we would have the dinner in some form or other and I was simply relieved that the emotional and physical ordeal was over.

I stood up stiffly, hoisted my pack on to my back and slowly started trudging down the mountain.

A week later in Buenos Aires airport we stood chatting in small groups by our untidy sea of 1200 kilos of equipment and possessions. The airport behaved like an airport, business men bought papers, policemen leaned idly against walls and passengers stood in queues hoping they would not be charged for their excess baggage.

Glen was not returning with us to Australia. Like a true sucker for punishment he was heading down to Chile for another expedition. His final comment summed up the whole mad affair.

'Chris, to have had a dinner party at six thousand eight hundred metres was an absolutely useless achievement but to have done it . . . was fantastic.'

EPILOGUE 1

The media coverage of the expedition far exceeded my wildest expectations. We had coverage in forty-one countries including fifty-five television spots, sixty-one newspaper and magazine articles and twenty-seven radio interviews, in places as far afield as Abu Dhabi, China, and Brunei. *The Guinness Book of Records* devoted a full page in their 1991 edition to the spectacular photograph of the Pisco lunch. The same photograph was used on the cover of the New Zealand, English, American and Canadian versions, it was almost a record in itself.

The Japanese became particularly excited. One TV crew flew down to film us in Australia and a rival channel flew Neil, Eddie, Ballantyne, Sally and me to Tokyo to appear on a show called 'Super People'. We expected to rub shoulders with the likes of Arnold Schwarzenegger and Carl Lewis but when we arrived in Tokyo the programme turned out to be a freak show. Our re-enactment of the North Head stunt looked very tame beside the world's youngest mother at nine years old, Mr Puniverse and his two-hundred kilo bride, a man who juggled chainsaws for a living and the four biggest breasts on the planet.

Ironically, Peru was almost the last country to give us

241

recognition. Nearly a year after we returned to Australia an article and accompanying photo hit the front page of the *Lima Times*.

A few months after the expedition Avril, Sally, Murf and I wanted to raise more money for the Heart Foundation. We decided to attempt to climb the equivalent height of walking from Lukla Airport (2890 metres above sea level) in Nepal to the summit of Everest (8848 metres) in a single day. We'd calculated that we could achieve this by walking up Sydney's highest skyscraper, the MLC Centre tower, thirty-one times over a fifteen hour period. Having climbed the 5950 metres within the time I felt tired but not half as exhausted as climbing just three hundred metres on Huascaran.

THE DOCUMENTARY

The documentary represents one record of the expedition. This book is another. Everyone sees events in different ways. The documentary focused on the angle Wolfgang wanted to portray — a group of stuck-up rich kids playing in South America, obsessed by etiquette and correct form, with the supposed love triangle and Charles Darwin connection as sub-themes.

It largely ignored the fact that we were total amateurs, enjoying an elaborate joke and braving considerable hardship and injury to achieve our goal. But as the producer pointed out, there are already hundreds of documentaries showing people struggling through far more dangerous conditions on Everest and in the Antarctic. So he felt justified in taking another angle.

To date the film has sold in Ireland, France and Germany. It can be no coincidence that these countries have traditionally never been warm friends with the English.

Wolfgang Ebert
Wolfgang's version of the documentary shows him climbing Huascaran. On close inspection however it turned out he had just cut various scenes featuring him from Pisco into the Huascaran section.

THE DOCUMENTARY CREW

Chris Hilton
Shortly after the expedition, Chris married. He is now directing his own documentary on Aboriginal culture.

Glen Singleman
Glen is planning Australia's first space mission on a tight budget and with a number of novel twists. Rockets are too complicated and far too expensive so he plans to ascend to 37 000 metres by balloon and parachute back to earth. Being a safety-minded person he has taken every possible precaution, including completing an extensive subaqua course, just in case he misses Australia on his descent.

Mike Dillon

> *I get a shiver down my spine every time I think about the expedition. Unfortunately I'll never fully get over malaria but at least I hold the world altitude record for the disease.*

Mike recently directed the documentary about Tim Macartney-Snape's expedition to walk from sea level to the summit of Everest.

THE GUIDES

All the guides, except Tenzing, stayed in Peru to continue working with Milton after the expedition. It is unclear exactly what happened but within a few months they had all either been fired or resigned.

Milton Sams
A few months after the expedition returned, a dispute developed between the documentary company and Milton

about US $800 Wolfgang had allegedly lent Milton. At the time of the dispute Milton was in possession of the dinner-party photographs and refused to return them to me, to stop the documentary company using them to promote the film. The situation deteriorated further when photographs taken by him were accidentally not credited in some newspaper articles.

Over the next three weeks my efforts to calm him failed. The night before Milton was due to return to South America I realised he had no intention of handing the photographs back. In a panic I consulted Alec Leopold, partner in the leading Sydney law firm Allen, Allen and Hemsley, who worked until the small hours to obtain, from the Supreme Court, an order that Milton hand the photographs over to the court.

Next morning, Alec, four policemen and I waited for him at Sydney airport. I had described Milton's manner and build and the policemen were therefore as nervous as me. They joked that if things turned nasty they might make a run for it.

Milton strode into the terminal effortlessly carrying two enormous packs and looking as formidable as usual. We plucked up courage and swarmed about him like a pack of terriers around a bear. We made no impression.

Milton swept the court order aside. 'Solicitors can't be trusted,' he told Alec.

He was advised by the sergeant that if he ignored the court order he could be arrested when he next entered the country.

'I don't care, go on arrest me, arrest me.'

Then he turned on me. 'You'll never see the photographs again,' he snarled, 'I've destroyed them.' He walked through customs and disappeared to Argentina.

Four months later we were alerted that Milton had slipped back into the country and he admitted he had not destroyed the photographs. An involved and extremely unpleasant legal battle followed. It transpired he had been under considerable stress before leaving for South America. There had been severe complications with his wife's pregnancy and his father-in-law was very ill.

After five months, $7000 of my own legal costs and a lot of heartache on all sides, the photos were returned. The book would go ahead after all.

I still do not understand Milton's behaviour. After all the work and effort he put into the expedition both on and off the mountain it seemed extraordinary to want to destroy the photographic record. Either he had grown to loathe the expedition or me. None of us have heard from him since and I assume he is still running his guiding business in South America.

Jim Nixon
At the time of writing Jim was rumoured to be in Nepal. It is unknown whether Techi is still with him.

Lorenzo, Britannion and the other **Hombres Supers**
I hope they are still getting work, given the difficult times in Peru.

Tenzing
Tenzing accompanied Mike Dillon on Tim Macartney-Snape's expedition to walk from sea level to the summit of Everest. He has since set up his own company in Kathmandu, Blue Dolphin White Water Rafting.

THE SOCIAL CLIMBERS

Avril Wynne

> I took a long time to recover after the expedition. I was exhausted for a couple of months. I think now I'm a more laid back and confident person than I was before the expedition. I'm also more vague. I think I lost a few brain cells on the top of Huascaran. If it wasn't the altitude, it must have been the Pisco Sours.

Avril gave up her job as an artificial inseminator on a

poultry farm and returned to stunt work for film and television. When the film industry is quiet, she works as a stop/go sign person with a road maintenance gang.

Ballantyne *(Eddie Ash)*

> *People keep telling me I was so close to the summit that I was as good as on it. I don't accept that. Anyone who likes to win will understand that I didn't make it. It was a terrible shame.*

Ballantyne became very depressed about not reaching the summit. His depression was made worse by his shoulder, which has never healed properly, ruling him out of further acrobatic work. This coincided with a slump in the film and television industry. He temporarily lost his self-confidence. But being a fighter, his fortunes soon changed for the better. He has started to get some television work and has taken up selling Electrolux vacuum cleaners door to door. Within a few months he became their number one salesman in northern NSW, just one more twist in his extraordinary life story.

Deirdre *Rawlings*

> *I have realised an enormous sense of my own worth and inner power. The experiences there have helped to reinforce my sense of responsibility for myself and my commitment to achieving my goals.*

Deirdre left Ansett and went for a six-month world tour, including trekking in Nepal.

Eddie *Moore*

> *The expedition awoke in me a dormant wonderlust, the opportunity and confidence to throw myself into uncontrolled and unknown situations. From this I've achieved a new understanding of my capabilities as well as a respect and love for mountains and mountaineering.*
>
> *The awesome beauty of a mountain sunset, the camaraderie and the physical challenges have left their indelible mark on me, enough to ensure a return visit to altitude.*

246

If nothing else I now have a few extraordinary fireside tales for my grandchildren.

Since the expedition Eddie has worked as an accountant in Australia's Snowy Mountains, a barman in an Austrian ski resort, a photographer covering the Nice Triathlon, a grape-picker in France and is, at the time of writing, a deckhand on a luxury yacht in the Caribbean.

Murf (Derek Murphy)

It was great to see the group reach their goal after so little training; the fact I was a ratbag probably helped. Peru was fantastic, the only problem with the expedition was that the whingeing poms had no bloody table manners.

Murf now owns an adventure clothing shop, *Rockcraft*, in Katoomba. He runs corporate survival weekends and is still the senior instructor at the Australian School of Mountaineering.

Neil Watson

The whole experience changed my life. I felt my priorities re-ordered. Success and material possessions remain important, but the expedition was a graphic illustration of something I knew but did not consciously acknowledge. Friendships, stopping to smell the flowers as it were, marvelling at sunsets and occasionally stripping away the social and material trappings of modern life are what really lead to contentment. The irony is it took an obsession with taking the trappings to the extremes, to bring this home to me.

Neil returned to his corporate finance job but soon resigned and went travelling. He met Trace in New Zealand, hiked through Thailand and finally went mountaineering in Nepal. Injury prevented him from climbing Mera Peak (6600 metres), so instead he claimed the title of 'the funniest man in Nepal'. Neil is now back in Australia working again in corporate finance. We are still close friends.

247

Sally Guyatt

*The rewards of mountaineering are hard to define. The views are
spectacular but you have to force yourself to look at them. You have
an enormous feeling of achievement but you cannot appreciate it
until you are down. Apart from a stunning selection of
photographs, the main thing I am left with is the feeling I am a
stronger and more confident person.*

*I'm getting married soon. Murf is designing the wedding dress,
Techi is doing the catering, the Shining Path are flying over
specially to be the welcoming committee and putting on an
impromptu fireworks display. Lorenzo will be the photographer
with the camera that disappeared from Milton's room and Milton
has kindly agreed to act as the master of ceremonies.*

Sally joined Coca-Cola Amatil as a computer analyst and
is talking about climbing another mountain.

Trace Taylor-Young

Shortly after the expedition Trace went to New Zealand
and immediately fell in love with the country.

*New Zealand is my sort of place. A small population, large spaces
and the most beautiful mountains. One day I shall live in Wanaka
with a view of the Mt Aspiring mountains and I shall be content.*

*But travelling is still in my system. I'd like to return to Nepal
— they were the first mountains to make me experience acute
emotional stirrings and I need to pay homage to them once again.*

*When I'm finding something really tough, I remind myself
that it has been considerably tougher on Huascaran and that is all
I need to get me there.*

When Trace is not working part-time as a travel agent
she is in the mountains. Her affinity has become an addic-
tion. She has climbed numerous peaks since the expedition;
spends a lot of time by herself trekking along the hundreds
of New Zealand tracks; rockclimbs; paraponts from the
tops of mountains and nude bungy jumps.

At the time of writing she is climbing in Nepal. She then

plans to spend a stint in Scotland before deciding where to settle down, in either Scotland or New Zealand, in the mountains of course.

Chris Darwin

As I walked down Huascaran I promised myself that I would never go high altitude mountaineering again. I think I was probably lucky to get out of the expedition alive. But now a year and a half later the reality is fading and I am left with romantic notions of mountaineering: the staggering beauty, the simplicity of the challenge and the sense of achievement.

The expedition was the most important event in my life. It has opened up a number of doors for me, none of which I have gone through. It taught me a lesson most people need to learn: we are all capable of so much more than we imagine. I am now a more confident person and I hope I am able to take a calmer attitude towards life.

Both Milton and Deirdre also taught me another lesson. I was not considerate to either of them during the expedition and I hope in the future I will be more sympathetic to others.

After the expedition both Trace and I were unhappy with the way things had ended between us. We met for a late-night picnic on top of Sydney Harbour Bridge. We sat huddled together in our duvet jackets on the top arch for five hours and discussed all aspects of the expedition. A number of interesting points emerged.

Clearly, everyone on the expedition now exhibited a higher level of personal confidence. But equally, it had unsettled people, and with their new-found confidence they were ready to leave their existing jobs and security in search of more adventure. Within a few months everyone, except for Murf and me, had left the jobs they had before the expedition and Neil, Eddie and Deirdre were travelling the world.

Another interesting outcome of the expedition was the

way in which enduring friendships were forged. Expeditions are always hotbeds of disagreement but no one ultimately took to heart things which were said and done under stress on the mountain. With the exception of one person, all the Social Climbers have become good friends.

Finally, Trace and I agreed that the mountains had somehow got into our blood. There is a legend that the world's highest mountains are the playgrounds of the gods. Furthermore, any mortal entering those ethereal heights will be tormented by mountain spirits until they return. This proved true for the Social Climbers. Within six months of the end of the expedition Neil, Murf, Deirdre and Eddie were either living in the mountains or spending prolonged periods there.

As dawn approached Trace and I climbed down the bridge and sadly went our separate ways. The next day she left to go and live in the mountains of New Zealand. I fished out my non-thermal black tie and returned to my old waiter's job at Darling Harbour.

EPILOGUE 2
FEBRUARY 1991

After finishing this book something has happened which necessitates a second epilogue.

A year and half after the expedition, Neil and I with four others went to New Zealand for Christmas. We hired a cottage in the mountains on the South Island. Trace joined us for a few days.

During a walk Trace made a comment that surprised me. 'The Social Climbers' expedition was the single most important event in my life,' she said. I never realised others felt the same as I did.

Trace was in two minds as what to do next in her life. After three years of travel she had become a virtuoso in the art of being an international mountain vagabond, living in remote mountain huts, youth hostels and under bridges. One side of her was terrified of giving up that lifestyle. Another side was niggling at her to settle down with her boyfriend.

By the end of Christmas she had decided on Johnnie but planned one final trip to Nepal, before going to Scotland to learn about small-farm holdings, goat-farming and bee-keeping.

Neil and I dropped Trace off in Omarama, on New

251

Zealand's South Island. She hugged both of us enthusiastically, bounced across the road and started hitchhiking. She looked so vulnerable, her slim frame standing beside her large pack. I noticed she was wearing the same melon print shorts as she wore on the day we spent together at Machu Picchu.

She waved to us with a warm smile as if to say, 'Off you go, I'll be all right.' As we drove south I hid my silent tears by pretending to look at the scenery.

A month and a half later, on 13 February 1991, Trace was trekking in Nepal in preparation for climbing Island Peak (6153 metres). She came across a small icefall and Trace, being Trace, decided to climb up above the track to get a photograph. She slipped and started sliding downwards. The friend she was travelling with said there was a moment when they caught each other's eye and both realised that Trace was not going to stop at the track. She plummeted down into a ravine, landing on the rocks.

Trace lay on her back, her arms outstretched, the back of her hand bleeding where it had hit the rocks, her face looking up at the mountains where she had first discovered her passion in life. All the members of the rescue team remarked how peaceful and serene she looked, thankfully indicating her death had been instantaneous.

SPONSORS AND PROJECT HELPERS

Major expedition sponsor
Ansett Airlines of Australia
Sir Peter Abeles
Tom Dery
Tony Hill
Mary Kinsella

Other Sponsors
Aerolineas Argentinas —
Flights to Buenos Aires and Lima
Keith Yorston

Ballantyne Chocolates —
Entertainmints
Andrew Ballantyne
John North

Thomas Hardy and Sons — Sir
James Champagne
David Woods
Andrew Barr
Cathy Somerville

Wilderness Expeditions — Travel
Agent
Allan Alcock
Sue Fear

Book Committee
Katharine Acland
Peter Adams
Kingsley Aikens

Neville and Peg Amy
Miles Bastick
Jessica Block
Rosemary Block
Paul Cockburn (*Design Field*)
Darwin family
Ari Droga
Daniel Droga
Josephine Elworthy
Dudy Gleeson-White
Bevis Dunn
Page Henty
Lyndel John
Ned Kelly
Caroline King
Clare McDonagh
Peter Talbot (Crow)
Keith Tuffley
Lyn White (*Design Field*)

Dining equipment and food
Whitehall — Candelabra
Dining equipment:
 Design Field —
 Volli Thorisson
 Paul Cockburn
 David Marriott
 Lyn White
 Local Vertical —
 Kent Miklenda

253

Mike Cook's Fish Works — Fish
Bradford Potter — Flowers
Guzzini — Glasses
Casamia Rino Cencigh — Louis
XIV chair
Decor — Plates
Rodd Silver — Silver

Documentary
Duracell — Batteries
Editors:
  Mike Balson
  Jenny Cornish
Canon — Fax Machine
Dick Dennison — Producer
Sian Butt — Production Assistant
Le Stage — Studio
The Dubb Shop — Video Editing

**Documentary Premiere —
Thomas Hardy and Sons**
Sir James Champagne
AFI Cinema
John Cooper's Sydney Foodshow —
Food
Camperdown Cellars — Glasses
Jessica Block — Co-ordinator
Kay de Lorenzo — Helper
Marge Keeble — Helper

Formal clothes
3M — Thermal lining for dresses
Grace Brothers Formal Hire —
thermal tails
Christopher Essex — thermal
balldresses
Governor Clothing — Waistcoats

Hangers On Club Committee
Kingsley Aikins
Eddie Ash
Jessica Block
Mary Bushby
Raz Darwin
Sarah Darwin
Shuna Darwin
Nicky Dyson
Ned Kelly
Kate Sainsbury
Tim Slater

Heart Foundation
Peter White
Paul Bruce
Jan Cosgrove
Isabell Brown
Mark Carmichael
Ross Bradford

Large charity donations:
  ANZ
  Allen, Allen and Hemsley
  Australian Geographic
  Freehill, Hollingdale and Page
  State Bank
  Towers Perrin
Heartstarters Ball — *Balliol Ball
Committee*
Proceeds to Heart Foundation
  Greg Bunting
  Robyn Elmlie
  Sally Guyatt
  Petar Vladeta

Miscellaneous assistance
HRH the Prince of Wales
The Guinness Book of Records
Wilderness Expeditions

**MLC Tower event: major
sponsor Ansett Airlines of
Australia**
Murf — Construction
Elizabeth Cask — Event manager
Lucozade — Energy drink
MLC Management:
  Lorelle Yee
  Ken Taylor
Comrent (Raymond Kerr-Lanson)
— Mobile phone
Steven Dupont — Photographer
Richard Wilson Lab —
Photographic display
Physiotherapists
  Simon MacKenzie Hicks
  Kelly Swindel
Tony Hill — *Ansett Publicity*
Reebok Energy Return Trainers —
Training shoes
Grace Brothers Formal Hire — Top
hats and tails

**Mountaineering equipment:
major sponsor Mountain
Equipment**
Macpac 'Torre' — Backpacks
Bolle — Dark glasses and goggles
J and H — Duvet jackets
Kathmandu — Fibrepile jackets
Johnson and Johnson — First aid
Panadol — Headache pills
Le Zinc — Suncream and sunblock
Peter Storm — Thermals
Reebok Energy Return Trainers —
Training shoes
Swatch Watches — Watches

North Head
Design Field and *Local Vertical* —
Art direction
Alls Barricades Hire — Barricades
Maizels — Casting
Sheraton Wentworth — Catering
Virginia Firth — Concept
development
North Head National Park —
Location
Comrent — Mobile phone rental:
Raymond Kerr-Lanson
Jonathan Chester — Photographer
Shelley Neller — Publicity
Pride Effects — Rig construction
Reaction Film Services — Safety
officer:
Burnie Ledger
Bridges Sharpe Consultants —
Sponsor organisation
Stunt Agency — Stunt
Avril Wynne
Grace Brothers Formal Hire — Top
hats and tails
Samuelsons Film Services —
Walkie-talkies
Cinesure — Walkie-talkie
insurance
Governor Clothing — Waistcoats
Houghton Wines — Wine

**Office Assistance, Equipment
and Stationery**
Accountants:
Karen McMillan

Tax Time — (John Sullivan)
Nigel Buchanan — Artist
Laser Graphics — Colour
separations

Concept development:
Jeff Barter
Peter Cudlipp
Al Darling
Justine Henwood
Torquil MacNeal
Kent Miklenda
Anne Clissold — Filing cabinet
Mike Tunica — Illustrator

Legal Advice:
Jessica Block — *Malleson
Stephen Jaques*
Ari Droga — *Clayton Utz*
Bevis Dunn
Alec Leopold — *Allen, Allen and
Hemsley*
Keith Tuffley — *Allen, Allen
and Hemsley*

Letterhead Design:
Lyn Pratt Wallace
Cato Design
R. T. Kelly — Letterhead printers

Office Assistance:
Jessica Block
Elizabeth Cask
Steven Jensen
Teresa Keating (*Irish Trade
Board*)
Karen MacMillan
Gloria Rodgers
Tim Slater
Kirsten Treharne
Mitchell Ross — Paper supplier
Design Field — Photocopying
Simon Bennetts — Photographer
Harold Droga — Sandwiches

Sponsorship:
Bridges Sharpe Consultants
Charles Kiefel
Michelle Murphy
Telecom — Telephones
Brother WP-1 — Wordprocessor

255

Writers:
John Amy
Torquil MacNeal
Neil Watson

Photographic equipment
Custom Darkrooms — Black and
white processing
Duracell Batteries
Fuji Colour Films
50ASA, 100 ASA, 400ASA
Fujichrome Professional
Ilford B and W Film
Pan F, FP4 and HP5
Photo Rentals Cameras
2 x Nikon FM2, 35mm-105
Nikkor, 80mm-200mm Nikkor,
Nikon 2X Teleconverter, Gossen
Profisystem Lightmeter

Peter Dambiec — Darkroom work
Richard Wilson Studios — Colour
Processing
(Assisted by *Colour
Development*)

Training
Dr Harrison — Doctor
Mountaineers:
Brian Harrison
Mick Pezet
Andrew Smith (Smut)
Peter Talbot (Crow)
Gillian Speirs — Physiotherapist

Swimming:
Harbourside Swim School
Spot Anderson
Steve and Kay de Lorenzo